D1594804

GERMAN - AMERICAN SETTLEMENT
IN AN OKLAHOMA TOWN

IMMIGRANT COMMUNITIES & ETHNIC MINORITIES IN THE UNITED STATES & CANADA: No. 56

ISSN 0749-5951

Series Editor: Robert J. Theodoratus
Department of Anthropology, Colorado State University

Continued at back of book

GERMAN - AMERICAN SETTLEMENT IN AN OKLAHOMA TOWN

Ecologic, Ethnic, and Cultural Change

TERRY J. PREWITT

AMS Press, Inc.
New York

F
704
038
P74
1989

Library of Congress Cataloging-in-Publication Data

Prewitt, Terry S.
    German American settlement in an Oklahoma town.

    (Immigrant communities & ethnic minorities in the United
States & Canada ; 56)
    Bibliography: p.
    Includes index.
    1. German Americans--Oklahoma--Okarche--Economic
conditions. 2. German Americans--Oklahoma--Okarche--Population.
3. Okarche (Okal.)--Population. 4. Okarche (Okla.)--Economic
conditions. I. Title. II. Series.
F704.038P74 1989   976.6·32   88-84003
ISBN 0-404-19466-4

All AMS books are printed on acid-free paper that meets the
guidelines for performance and durability of the Committee on
Production Guidelines for Book Longevity of the Council on
Library Resources.

AMS PRESS
56 East 13th Street
New York, N. Y. 10003, U.S.A.

MANUFACTURED IN THE UNITED STATES OF AMERICA

TABLE OF CONTENTS

LIST OF TABLES

LIST OF MAPS

LIST OF FIGURES

Page

PREFACE

This book had its origin in the interdisciplinary academic setting of the social science programs at the University of Oklahoma in the middle 1970s. As a graduate student recently returned from Germany, I divided my studies between the culture history of Europe and the cultural ecology emphasis of the Oklahoma anthropology department. At that time, the department had close ties to the disciplines of geography and history, marked especially by cooperation in an annual frontier studies symposium. I also pursued studies of general system theory through the sociology faculty. When I became aware of the town of Okarche as a potential subject of study, I was already preparing proposals for dissertation work in Austria. But, the opportunity to integrate the topics of demography, cultural ecology, and social system analysis in an American frontier context seemed too great to resist. Okarche provided a context for enhancing our understanding of an important,

recent cultural transformation through the application
of ecological perspectives to historical evidence.

Although in 1979 I vigorously defended the "anthropological" nature of this work, today I consider it more
geographic or sociological. My intent was to capture in
a complex social field some of the cultural regularities
and historical continuities which mark a community,
providing a clear identity for its inhabitants. The
work draws mainly upon documentary evidence on German
heritage in Okarche, though I accomplished limited
"ethnographic" interview work in the town. The point
which strikes me most now is that the language I used
for description and analysis takes this work out of the
realm of history, or even perhaps of "ethnohistory." I
am sure I would write it differently today, even if my
concern with explanation of events over understanding of
individuals has not changed that much. My writing has
changed as research interests have broadened for me,
especially in taking up a semiotic framework for the
study of cultural symbols.

I continue to be involved in demographic studies. Indeed, I have pursued similarly-based historical and demographic research in northeast Oklahoma and in Ireland since completing the Okarche study. The emphasis of the more recent work has been more ethnographic and historical, though built on a very similar demographic-economic analysis. Most important, I have attempted to develop a more humanistic style of writing. But this book on Okarche remains useful for those who are not put off by its several layers of jargon. It also demonstrates how rich the U.S. German data can be for community studies of the late 19th and early 20th centuries.

I have left the manuscript more or less in its original form. Some minor rewriting fixed grammatical problems of a major sort, but I resisted doing all that might have enhanced the clarity of the original arguments. This is because I feared a fuller rewrite might cause more problems than it solved, including possibly losing the sense of the argument on heritage. Some work is better left unrevised, even at risk of losing a few readers. The readings of Robert Theodoratus and Jeff Eighmy upon which the manuscript was selected for inclusion in the AMS Press series give me confidence that many will find this study of Okarche useful in approaching similar problems. I want to especially thank Robert Theodoratus for his interest in the work.

Many people have contributed to this book in substantial ways, and it is with great pleasure, tempered in places with a touch of sadness, that I note their various contributions here. The writing of this work has spanned three institutional affiliations and a multitude of influences, so I hope my simple listings will not seem too curt.

Central to this work is my whole graduate experience, and so my first debt is to my colleagues in the Department of Anthropology at the University of Oklahoma. To Stephen I. Thompson and Joseph W. Whitecotton my debt is tremendous. They have both given me encouragement and guidance, ecology, symbols, and friendship. Robert E. Bell, William E. Bittle, the late Ralph Cooley, and Richard Pailes also gave of themselves throughout my research, providing direction, criticism, and support. This book reflects my conversation and debates with a particular collegial cohort--Bob Stahl, Greydon Doolittle, Jane Johnson, Stan Johnson, Tim Baugh, Bob Rhoades, Mike Birchall, Dan Reff, Kent Buehler, Dennis Wiedmann, Robert Nespor, Judy Whitecotton, Craig Gerlack, Charlie Gourd, Kay Fagan, Carolyn Pool, Gerry Williams, Chris Lintz, Ann Jordan, and many more--who formed my intellectual context in the 1970s.

I must also express my gratitude to James Bohland for introducing me to Okarche, Leonard Jordan for guiding me to general system theory, and Morris Opler for his time in many conversations which gave me perspectives on symbolic analysis. William Savage and Jerome O. Steffen have helped me in approaches to frontier studies and Oklahoma history, through both informal conversations and suggested reading and sources.

Several of my colleagues in the Department of Anthropology at the University of Houston discussed aspects of my Okarche work with me. Russ Reid made many suggestions on demographic approaches and general ecological theory, and Norris Lang read drafts of several of the chapters. Pauline Kolenda and Michael Agar helped me grapple with some formative notions on symbols, and so indirectly contributed to my writing of Chapter V. Barbara Liss read and critiqued Chapter IV, and provided many helpful comments on the general direction of the book. Additionally, Garrick Bailey and Pat Blessing of the University of Tulsa have provided encouragement during the completion of the study--their support is greatly appreciated.

Ms. Karen Haworth drew all of the illustrations, and aided in preparing the final draft, checking citations, and proof-reading the manuscript. Ricki Rubenstein and Susan Miller typed early drafts of the work with help also from Denise Mason.

Finally, I would like to thank the many people of Okarche, the Federal Records Center in Forth Worth, the

Oklahoma Historical Society, the University of Oklahoma special library collections staff, all of whom helped in the collection of information contributive to this study.

The manuscript preparation for this book was accomplished through the work and support of several individuals. Mrs. Connie Works typed the manuscript and prepared several working versions for editing. Ms. Renee Dykxhoorn performed an early editorial reading of the copy, and helped organize the illustrations for production. Ms. Karen Haworth helped me prepare new illustrations from the original drawings. Declan Patterson and Louise Walsh prepared the subject index. Finally, I am indebted to Instructional Media Services and Charles Meister for help in preparing the illustration masters. Of course, I want to thank again all of the people who helped me during the time I completed the work.

GERMAN-AMERICAN SETTLEMENT IN AN OKLAHOMA TOWN:

ECOLOGIC, ETHNIC, AND CULTURAL CHANGE

CHAPTER I

INTRODUCTION

THE PROBLEM

The town of Okarche, Oklahoma, was founded in 1892 during the opening of the Cheyenne-Arapaho Reservation to non-Indian settlers. Although the Okarche area was settled by European-American families of quite diverse backgrounds, very early in its history it became a center dominated by German-speaking families. By the early 1940's, the preponderance of families associated with Okarche were of German heritage, many of them representing children and grandchildren of original settlers. Thus, an initially small group of foreign-born and first-generation German-Americans achieved success in Okarche, ultimately displacing a large sector of population of other backgrounds in both farming and town-associated pursuits.

One might think that "German" identity would play an important part in such a situation, and indeed it does in some respects. But the German-speaking settlers of Okarche really had much less common heritage than is suggested by the popular label "German." Moreover, the notions that "Germans are better farmers" or have a greater "love of the land"--themes often propounded in popular literature and some anthropological circles--do not hold up under close scrutiny (see especially Jordan 1966). Nonetheless, Germans prevailed in Okarche. Therefore, this dissertation is an investigation of the part played by "heritage" in bringing about the successes of those families who came to dominate and control Okarche during the first half-century after its founding. The central point of analysis involves tracing the ties between a changing population and changing sets of symbolic references I call "tradition."

CONCEPTUAL STRUCTURE

Heritage, if it is to be viewed as a "causal" agent in social continuities or change, required identification in social praxis. Such an identification is accomplished through reference to "tradition." Both "heritage" and "tradition" refers to elements of the background of individuals. The term "heritage" refers to the elements of cultural orientation based in general features of prior familial association--places of origin, language, and economic background. But "tradition" refers to the belief systems surrounding elements drawn from heritage, especially as they guide human associations ("tradition" relates to the "aggregations of symbols" of Whitecotton's 1976 discussion of ethnicity; see also Barth 1969: 9-38). Therefore, the terms are used to distinguish levels of common background, one stressing simple individual identification and the other stressing social self-identification. It is recognized in the distinction that although two individuals may come from quite common backgrounds, and therefore share common heritage, they may move in quite different social circles, share in different self-identifying concepts, relate to their common backgrounds in different ways, and even be drawn into competition.

To the extent that the people of Okarche are tied to German background, the interest of this dissertation is in the nature of German heritage and tradition--in other words, this work is directed toward the study of "ethnicity" in Okarche. However, the term "ethnic" has been given popular connotations in recent years which make "ethnicity" an undesireable word for the kind of work attempted here. Further, there is lack of precision (Ruth 1976) and difference of opinion as to an appropriate definition of "ethnicity" for historical and anthropological work (cf. Hale 1975: 201-3; Whitecotton 1976). Ethnic groups are usually associated with some specific cultural content--something directly

observable, culturally distinctive, symbolically fixed
or immutable. From this perspective, an "ethnic group"
exists because of its culture, and membership is based
upon more or less ascriptive rules. German culture,
then, becomes the basis for assessing an "ethnic"
Germanness--the situation of having enclaves of people
practicing German culture outside Germany--and people
become "ethnic Germans" by being born into a particular
identifiable group (an "aggregation of people," see
Whitecotton 1976) or by becoming accepted in it.

It follows from such a position, especially in the
wake of national character studies, that when the
cultural forms associated with an ethnicity change, the
ethnicity ceases to exist. If "German cultural practice" gives way, then "ethnic Germanness" is undermined.
If we accept the most extreme statements of culturally-
defined ethnicity, then anything short of substantial
"German" cultural baggage does not seem to suffice as
authentic. Following Whitecotton (1976) and Barth

(1969), I believe that such an approach to ethnicity is totally inadequate. It serves only to "identify" groups rather than to provide information as to their nature. Indeed, strict cultural definitions of ethnicity become nearly as extreme as that literature of the "national character" era which, even if short of lending understanding of our enemies, at least clearly set them apart from ourselves. There may be some justification for viewing the focus of local "tradition" as a reflex of national attitudes toward groups of particular background--in this case involving changes of orientation with the two World War periods (see Ruth 1976: 12). But there is no justification for presuming that (a) any identification with a background implies full knowledge or acceptance of particular cultural content, or (b) a substantial cultural correspondence is necessary between the "tradition" of a group and the background to which it relates as a formerly extant cultural system, in order to warrant the identification of an ethnic group.

Of course, ethnic groups do exist because of culture, but they do not depend upon any particular cultural content. It is the essentially arbitrary, highly expressive, symbolically and materially adjustable aspects of culture which define an ethnicity within a cultural arena or cultural field (see Bailey 1969, on "political fields" and the concept of "arena"). For that matter, all levels of human groups are so defined. The changes of cultural content attendant to the evolution of an ethnic or group association make descriptive tasks difficult at times. But these same changes should also be the central point of analysis, for they are the medium of adaptation of the human species (Bailey 1969: 196-202; Barth 1969; Geertz 1963; Eisenstadt 1969, in his treatments of "free-floating" resources and "autonomous goals"--see especially note pages 18-20, 26-8; Cole and Wolf 1974: 286; Redfield 1950: 155-78).

The notion of "tradition" provides a way to formally recognize the changeable and sometimes arbitrary

relations of groups of individuals to their respective
backgrounds. The idea of "heritage" enables the recognition that all people have an identifiable cultural
background, whether it serves as a focal point for the
individual or not. These rather common terms bridge the
crucial points of our concern with "ethnicity," then, if
it is conceived in a manner which allows social continuities in the absence of cultural continuities.

If culture has adaptive value at all, that value
must in part be based upon flexibility (Rappaport 1974;
see Cole and Wolf 1974: 284-5). The terminology of this
dissertation with regard to ethnicity is intended to
recognize such flexibility. And it should be emphati-
cally stated that "tradition" is focused into time and
is highly interpretive of historical cultural conditions. The "symbols" of tradition are compositions,
highly selective in material and forms of expression,
that relate current situations to elements of the past
(see Levi-Strauss 1966: 233-5). As such they are

constantly changing (at least in those societies Levi-
Strauss would call "hot"). Thus, precedents in the past
for conditions of the present are sought in historical
revision, or allowed to lapse out of memory when they
get in the way. This form of change is mainly concentrated on what elements to draw into the fray. On
another level of change, however, tradition is sometimes
refocused--it is allowed to embrace entirely new
elements, the reformulation of identity also giving a
group new character.

If there were people in Okarche today who were
"culturally German," one might argue that ethnicity in a
direct cultural sense was responsible for the present
family composition of the community. This is not the
case, however, and so from a strictly cultural perspective, German identity can have nothing to do with
present population composition in Okarche. This does
not negate the unlikely circumstance that the overwhelming majority of Okarche's present households are of

German heritage, when German people were only a fraction
of the original population in the immediate vicinity of
the town. Much of the following material, therefore,
attempts to account for the nearly exclusively "German"
population of present-day Okarche through social
continuities, recognition of cultural changes, and
presentation of the key points of demographic development. Although limited proposals are entertained which
outline the specific cultural differences between German
and non-German segments of Okarche's population, my
major arguments relate to the demographic, economic, and
social information which links the present population to
organized groups of the pioneer era of Oklahoma.

In approaching this work, I have primarily sought
local causes for the cultural changes and major shifts
of population which characterize Okarche's past. In
particular, attention is given to economic conditions in
Okarche as they favored or impeded the continuity of
technological practices, and demographic conditions as

they have established families on the land in stable techno-economic adjustments. The argument that social continuities represent manifestations of ethnicity is similar to Williams' (1978) arguments concerning social and cultural definitions of ethnicity for Welsh groups of the Lower Chubut Valley, Argentina. The Germans of Okarche have mainly changed from "culturally defined" to "socially defined" groups. But I have also stressed the reorientation of "tradition" as an important part of this process. That is to say, changes in elements of tradition by a group serve to reset the limits of permissible actions or associations, and thus operate directly to conserve or capture "resources" of the sociocultural system. The ability of a group to culturally redirect itself, then, is the means through which the continuity of social identity is attained-- plus ca change, plus c'est la meme chose.

THE SOCIOLOGICAL SETTING

Historians, geographers, and a few anthropologists
have turned to a common field of observation in the
study of "pioneer colonization" (Thompson 1973), an
orientation closely allied to "frontier" studies on a
larger areal scale (Turner 1961; Hartz 1964; Miller and
Steffen 1977). "Community" and small regional studies
have taken on new form in this area of research,
especially including demographic and technological
studies of small pioneer groups throughout the world.
The work is usually local--it lacks the hard reliance on
broad statistical presentations common to much of
contemporary social science--but it affords us a critical medium for the observation of major systemic transformations in relatively short periods of time. The
demographic techniques of "pioneer" studies differ somewhat from regional and national scale demographic
approaches, mainly in their concentration upon family

history and total population presentation. These techniques have been developed particularly in history, and are important to the reformation of colonial American history (see Powell 1963, Greven 1970, Lockridge 1970). This study is grounded in similar direct demographic approaches, including the use of techniques known in anthropology from recent work by Hammel and Laslett (1974) and Kertzer (1977).

The study of frontiers is important for a number of reasons. As a social situation the "frontier" provides a "laboratory" for the study of cultural and social change as general processes (Thompson 1973). In addition, the study of frontiers may allow more specific treatment of culture-demographic relationships than is possible in other social contexts. Well-established or "mature" communities may seem essentially "boundary maintaining" or "homeostatic" in their operation, whether viewed historically or in contemporary settings (see Homans 1942 on "equilibrium" systems; Cole and Wolf

1974 on "homeostasis and ecology" as an anthropological
orientation). That is, even in complex societies change
often proceeds slowly, making its recognition so difficult that it casts the observer into a dilemma of
descriptive scale. Some workers prefer a "synchronic"
approach in the interest of logical or structural
presentation of the social system, while others attached
themselves to broad time-frames and the transformations
of the system. The description of precise logical
structures relies on different forms of detailed work
than does the description of the "diachronic system.

But the scale of events on the frontier--the pace of
change--is right for detailed scrutiny and the resolu-
tion of logical structure and historical events. The
dynamics of change are best seen where they are boldly
manifested. The essentially adaptive quality of culture
is best seen when adaptation is taking place. The
quality of struggle for existence in human life is most
clearly understood when the struggle is pronounced. It

is these elements of the frontier situation which provide strategic advantage for the study of human biocultural adaptation and change.

Thus, the study of Okarche is done more in the spirit of frontier and pioneer research than from the perspective of anthropological community studies. The view point toward human relationships is especially linked to "familial" considerations through the demographic elements of the work. The demographic treatment is also ecological, but it is specifically not framed from the theoretical perspectives of "cultural ecology" (Steward 1955, Netting 1977) or the "culture-materialism" of Harris (1968). The only directly ecological materials and methods of this work are derived from Odum (1971) and from the perspective of general system theory.

The solution of the questions posed in his dissertation, although primarily based on demographic patterns in time, is a direct product of complex relations

posited between factors of economy, environment, technology, symbols, communication, and most important,
group identity. These factors are common grist of
"functional" and "ecological" approaches of anthropology, but the general-system-theoretic perspective is
taken in the hope of avoid some of the pitfalls of
strictly "functional" and "conflict" perspectives of the
social sciences. In the body of this work materials on
the demography, economy, and social units of Okarche are
drawn into an essentially historical account. In the
final chapter, the substantive results of the work are
reviewed and several broad theoretical points are made
relating to frontier population dynamics, the intensity
of ethnic identification, and the general relations
between symbolic and material realms of cultural
process. These broader arguments form the last three
sections in the conclusion of the dissertation, and are
presented in both a summary form and in terms which may
disgruntle those who have no commitment to general

system theory. The sections are presented, nonetheless, in order to allow some of the empirical generalizations of this study of Okarche to have meaning in broader sociocultural contexts, specifically in a range of "frontier" situations including urban systems.

Inasmuch as the bulk of this work is "historical" in its orientation, it is also necessary to indicate that I am aligned with numerous contemporary workers who use history as a vehicle to make certain anthropological, sociological, geographic, or otherwise "scientific" points. I believe that a history carries a theoretical message, in part, directly stated and, in part, manifested in its organization. The situation of Okarche is appropriate to the study of processes of social and cultural change, demographic change, economic change--human evolution--although it might be studied for many other reasons. But Okarche becomes of intrinsic interest to me only in a humanistic sense which is, after all is said and done, not the reason I have

engaged in this work. Still, I feel obliged to attempt
to project something of the feeling and orientation of
the people of Okarche at points along the way. At no
point in this work, however, do I feel obliged to
provide an "ethnic" history or "ethnohistory."

DEVELOPMENT OF THE STUDY

Most anthropological work is presented in the form
of reconstructed logic. Formal arguments which were
arrived at through a sometimes confused and essentially
inductive process are presented as through they were
perceived by the investigator in deductive terms from
the very beginning. It is easy to get the impression
that the subject at hand thrust itself upon the observer
as a well-defined "system" or "structure." The initiated fieldworker understands this shortcoming of the
written report.

But sometimes it is useful to review, briefly, the actual logical steps through which a problem developed in the course of research. This is as much an aid to the author as to the reader, for it provides a context in which the rather dogmatic arguments attributable to "style" are softened. Therefore, in the following few pages, I attempt to relate the major stages in the development of questions pertaining to Okarche. This discussion should make it clear that the nature and scope of empirical questions about Okarche changes as the work progressed, although the basic question of the work remained the same. It should also be clear that some of the theoretical conclusions submitted in the final chapter are a product of the long term interests of the author and the situations in which this dissertation was written.

The central question of the Okarche study was present at the outset: What part did German identity play in the successes of those families that came to

dominate and control the community in the first half-
century after its founding? It is assumed in this
question that German identity plays some part in the
changing population composition of Okarche. Indeed,
when I first became aware of Okarche, my work was
directed toward the obvious continuity of German
families from the pioneer period to the present. Therefore, early in the investigation, I pursued leads to
cultural content that might have conferred advantage
upon the German population. Within a short time, however, the lack of strong German cultural content in
present day Okarche began to cast doubt upon the notion
that Germans were successful by virtue of cultural
distinctiveness. Of course, the modern situation does
not preclude a strong German cultural commitment in the
past, but while Okarcheans seem very aware of their
background, they also seem to know little of the
cultural intricacies of that background. And the
documents on Okarche's past indicate a major change of

cultural orientation from a predominately German-American direction, so that even by the time of the First World War "Germanness" was much less manifest than in the early years of settlement.

Yet, even though German culture waned, the number of German families in census materials, burial populations, and the present population increased. Thus, at the point of research in which primary data on German families and community demography were being compiled, it became obvious that more attention must be paid to community organization and the symbols and identifying concepts surrounding groups within the community. It was at this point in the work that the distinction between heritage and tradition was applied to the Okarche population.

This shift of emphasis involved a step away from what had initially been conceived as an essentially ecological problem toward a more direct study of social units and symbols. That is, a culture-ecological

explanation of the success of Germans might rest in the
techno-environmental distinctiveness of an "ethnic"
population. In such an argument, differential success
of groups might be based upon material conditions.
Lacking such material differences, an alternative
hypothesis involving social distinctiveness was posited
and data pertinent to the hypothesis were sought. These
data were of two forms. First, material and demographic
information concerning the composition, continuity, and
identity of social groups in the community were organized from the materials already under study. The
association of families within these groups were particularly sought. Second, information was gathered
concerning corporate actions and informal actions of
groups. From this work, the notion of "tiered" German
identification in Okarche was developed, wherein
individuals were identified at one level with a congregation and on another level as simply "German."

Thus, parallel empirical questions began to emerge around which this dissertation was ultimately written. The first set of questions has to do with the demographic conditions in Okarche during settlement and the place of German groups in the settlement process. A second set deals with economic actions of groups and the development of the rural-oriented community economic pattern of the modern era, with particular attention to potential differences between German and non-German groups. Some of the information brought to bear on these questions indicates that German cultural orientation diminished as a force in the community, while other information documents the strong persistence of German social units.

These key materials are discussed in Chapters III, IV, and V. The specific empirical questions I have attempted to answer are as follows: What was the size and composition of the Okarche population, including both town and rural components, during the period from

1889 through 1940? What major trends in population
dynamics can be identified during the period? More
specifically, what was the timespan of German-American
entry into the Okarche area? How did early settlers
organize their agricultural and business pursuits? What
kinds of economic enterprise can be identified, under
pioneer conditions and after, as having had either
short- or long-term prospects of success? What social,
geographic, and economic factors mediated success and
failure of the economic strategies which were practiced?
How did individuals acquire their initial land, and
under what conditions were subsequent additions of land
made? What was the composition of households, and how
did that composition vary over time? To what extent
were different households related through kinship or
other prior associations at the time of settlement?
What voluntary associations were established by the
people during the early years of settlement, and which
of these continued long after the homestead period? To

what extent are there patterns of family organization,
interpersonal association, and economic orientation
which are attributable to heritage? More directly, what
elements of life in early Okarche are closely patterned
after organizations common to particular areas of Europe
or the United States from which Okarche pioneers came?
What patterns of activity in Okarche were established in
direct response to the Oklahoma environment, but can not
be said to have roots in individual or collective background of the settlers? Finally, and most important,
how do all of these factors interrelate in determining
the directions and rate of social change in the community of Okarche?

Beyond these questions lie other considerations.
For the most part, the significance of Okarche does not
rest in its particular manifestations of German "ethnicity" or the specifics of its economic development and
organization. Rather, the Okarche case tell us something about ethnic identifications in general, and about

the relations of ethnicity to economic and population
stress. I believe that the frontier setting of the
Okarche study, in part, led me to the kinds of generalizations offered in Chapter VI. However, much of the
argument concerning the dynamics of ethnicity in
frontier settings applies also to certain urban systems.
Thus, a similarity is suggested between "frontier" and
"urban" population dynamics, as well as the nature of
ethnicity in the two kinds of systems. These matters
are the results of my long time interests in system
analysis, the processes which characterized the Okarche
case, and the fact that much of the conclusion was
written, fortuitously, while I was also directly
involved with several scholars with specialties in urban
and applied anthropology. Thus, while some of the
concluding sections of this dissertation may seem like
an afterthought, they appear so mainly because of the
introduction of arguments about urban systems and
regional development, and, perhaps, because of the shift

to a quite different style of presentation. Yet the arguments are essential if one is to understand the theoretical relationships between ethnicity and symbols on the one hand, and demography or economic considerations on the other. It is important to me that Okarche be understood in terms of general processes of social action and change, not in terms of the historical particulars of the case.

The study of Okarche developed, then, first as an empirical statement set against the background of a Oklahoma settlement, and second, as a theoretical statement about demography and ethnicity in frontier and urban systems, or rather, geographic systems involving rapid population turnover, as we shall see. The background--Chapter II--was indeed written first, and represents the kernel statement of the substantive issues to be incorporated in the dissertation. The organization of the materials benefited from two major adjustments. First, the chapter on economics was placed

before the chapter on social units (Chapters IV and V).
Second, the sections of Chapter VI were rearranged to
place them in their present order. These changes from
the original order of data and argument allow the reader
to move from the strongly substantive early chapters to
the more abstract final chapters. At least, demographic
information seems more solid than contentions about
ethnic identity. However, a particular benefit of this
organization is that the reader may with little diffi-
culty disregard the last three sections of the conclusion and not lost any of the substantive argument of the
work.

CHAPTER II

THE SETTING: OKLAHOMA AND THE OKARCHE PIONEERS

ECOLOGICAL BACKGROUND

The area in which the town of Okarche was founded was originally a rolling tall-grass prairie, dominated by a rather lush growth of little bluestem, side-oats grama and bluegrama (see Kuchler 1964). Under the grass was a well developed, rich, dark soil and clayey sub-soils on a parent surface stratum of clayey Red Beds (see Gray and Galloway 1959 for a general treatment of Oklahoma soils; also see Oklahoma Water Resources Board 1975, Section II: 12-12a). These were considered prime agricultural lands; more potentially productive than the Sandsage-Bluestem and Buffalo Grass prairies of regions farther west, and more easily broken out for farming than the Cross-Timbers and Oak-Hickory savannahs to the east (Map 1). The locality expressed only moderate

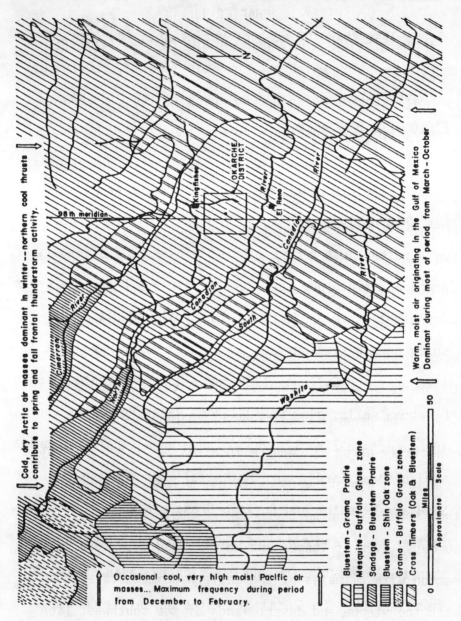

Map 1. The Okarche district, located in
its context of major geographic zones in central
and northwest Oklahoma (after Küchler 1964).

relief, less than 100 feet of variation below the
terrace crest on which the town was located, gently cut
by small streams which flowed north to the Cimarron
River. These streams were intermittently fed by an
average of 30 inches in yearly precipitation, most of it
concentrated in the Spring and the early Fall thunder-
storms (Oklahoma Water Resources Board 1975, Section II:
1). Storms on the prairie lands produced then, as they
do today, broad extremes of day-to-day, and even year-
to-year, variation. There could be too much wind and
water or not enough, particularly as considered against
the needs of a predominantly agricultural community.
Still, the general conditions of climate were not
especially harsh as compare to areas north and east of
Oklahoma. Winters were certainly milder and shorter
than those of the northern plains-prairie country, and
summers, even if longer and hotter, had much more in
common with climates of the eastern United States than
with the steppe and desert lands of the southwest (see

Haurowitz and Austin 1944: 204-11, for a standard,
general treatment of North American climate).

Indeed, if there was a resource potential which the
Okarche area lacked, it was biotic variety. There were
few trees which might offer ready sources of building
materials or fuel. Such trees as were in the area grew
small and were scattered along larger stream channels.
The vast majority of minor plants available were
grasses--big bluestem, western wheatgrass, buffalo
grass--and a number of wildflowers and other forbs
(Kuchler 1964). The ecosystem of the prairie was highly
specialized then, manifesting relatively few species
each with very large populations, so that any major
impact on one element of the regime could easily be felt
by the whole (Geertz 1963: 12-37; D. Harris 1969:
4-5).

The classical animal dominants of this region are
well known. First among them was the bison, everywhere
prominent and central for several thousand years to

articulations of people to the midcontinental environment (see Willey 1966: 42-51; Spencer and Jennings
1977: 316-8; Lowie 1963: 15-8, 205-18). Later came
the domestic companion of the bison, the horse, which
after its introduction in the early 1700's quite rapidly
attained very large populations (Lowie 1963: 42-6;
Oliver 1962). The horse strongly influenced the lives
of humans on the Plains, entrenching them solidly in a
very efficient, but specialized orientation toward bison
hunting (Oliver 1962). Thus, larger numbers of people
subsisted in relative bounty while concentrating on a
single major component of the natural resource base. At
a later time, however, there was an easy disruption of
the equestrian hunters through the simple, systematic
extermination of the bison herds, rendering the Native
Americans of the Plains dependent upon the United States
within a very few years.

These events occurred well before the opening of
Oklahoma Territory, but the same principles of

ecoligical specialization remain crucial to our under-
standings of later patterns of human endeavor. For a
time, Texas cattlemen could exploit the grasslands of
Oklahoma as a rapid and inexpensive route for movement
of large herds to northern markets, and as a range which
increased herd poundage enroute (McReynolds 1964:
250-66). This arrangement also was easily disrupted in
a few years. The "cattle frontier," resting as it did
on requirements of plentiful open range and volume
production, fell victim to the same economic expansion
from which it had sprung after the Civil War--the final
settlement of the great, dreary middle of the continent.
There began to arrive on the scene a large population of
more sedentary orientation, and another great transformation of the prairie was underway (McReynolds 1964:
279-89; Rister 1942).

As the pioneers of Okarche first looked across the
grasslands they would homestead, they stood in time at a
sort of "ecological threshold"--representing, in part,

the beginning of a new specialized regime. But this was to be, ultimately, a controlled regime of much greater magnitude than any perpetrated before through human activity. We should note again that "action" in a specialized ecosystem is almost always conducted on a grand scale. We might say, the orchestration is simple but produced with great fortissimo. But this would be insufficient, in and of itself, to account for the kind of transformation of which the Okarche pioneers were a part. What gave the settlement era its unique and lasting qualities was the condition that human actions in the system did not necessarily fall into harmony, initially at least, with the existing natural order of the region. In fact, some human actions of the settlement era ran totally counter to the specialized biological organization of former years. Yet they persisted in the short run, and so set into motion the massive irreversible adjustments which meant the final end to the tall-grass prairie.

What would ultimately replace the old order was not immediately evident. Perhaps the most dramatic change after the Oklahoma openings was the radical increase in human population density, especially in its context of individual land ownership. Population density has probably never exceeded one person per square mile during the presettlement periods (see Lowie 1963: 11-14). However, the rural population of the Okarche area exceeded thirteen persons per square mile after the Cheyenne-Arapaho opening (derived from correlated information in the Oklahoma Tract Book, the Oklahoma Territorial Census, 1890, and the Twelfth Census of the United States,1900). This figure is typical of the Unassigned Lands and eastern sections of the Cheyenne-Arapaho reservation, and, if city population were included, it would be even higher. Thus, human population factors alone provided a great deal of the "kick" which, apart from matters of technological impact, began pushing the prairie system in a new direction. From an ecological perspective, what is paradoxical and interesting about the settlement situation is the diversity of the pioneer population. The cultural "baggage" the people brought with them was far from uniformed. It was technologically implemented in many different ways, and the whole population was divided into a multiplicity of groups. There was great human "variety," and, to a degree, the people attempted to enforce a similar state of affairs on the total biotic sphere. Thus, the transformation of the ecosystem was from a specialized system to one more generalized, with great fluidity and variety.

However, generalized conditions were not to endure, for both economic and ecological reasons. The economic causes involved the development of the wheat industry in the central United States, especially its extension into the southern plains, even though this development does not account for the local play of factors which brought about particular stable populations in particular places. Indeed, Oklahoma wheat production was not great until about 25 years after settlement (Haystead and Fite 1955: 185-7).

We might better look at the factors which enabled some Oklahoma farmers to become successful in the wheat market before citing it as a primary cause of the total developmental situation. The impact of wheat specialization followed the major impacts of local environmental constraints on small farm operators in Okarche and elsewhere--constraints which acted on the artificial and highly vulnerable position of individuals on a landscape with unfamiliar properties, few local options for relocation, and a rudimentary system of communication.

THE INITIAL SETTLER POPULATION

The opening of the unassigned lands of Oklahoma in 1889 brought together settlers from Kansas, Missouri, Iowa, Texas, Illinois, Indiana, Tennessee, and most of the other states and territories to the north and east. Among these people were a few foreign-born Americans and some recent immigrants from Europe and Canada (see Hall 1975 for a general treatment of European immigrants to Oklahoma). Within four years, the Cheyenne-Arapaho lands and the Cherokee Outlet had also been opened, bringing more settlers from all parts of the country. This later settlement, as well as the subsequent migrations to Oklahoma, included a higher proportion of foreign-born persons, over 35 percent of whom were German-speaking (Hale 1975: 182-3). After the turn of the century, the Oklahoma German-speaking population was concentrated in the north-central parts of the state, especially in Oklahoma, Canadian, and Garfield counties

(Hale 1975: 184). These people have been the subject
of interest of a few scholars over the years, although
there is little in the way of "German-American" literature pertaining to Oklahoma (however, see Willibrand
1950, 1951; Pulte 1971 also offers brief comments on
limited linguistic studies of Germans in Oklahoma).
Recent work by historians and anthropologists reflects a
growing orientation toward studies of European "ethnic"
groups in Oklahoma, and the interest has been mirrored
in popular literature on the settlement of the region (a
key point of Hale 1975 concerns the need for historical
work on ethnic groups in Oklahoma; see also Naramore
1973, Ruth 1976).

Okarche, today a town of about 800 people, is
located approximately in the center of the German-
American concentration in north-central Oklahoma, on the
boundary between Kingfisher and Canadian counties. it
is a visible German-American "ethnic enclave" only in a
very general sense. The populations of the center and

surrounding rural areas are composed predominantly of people of German-speaking heritage. Yet on a superficial level, Okarche is rather "typical" or rural Oklahoma. There is nothing particularly unusual about the visual appearance of the town which dramatically sets it apart from other rural centers. It is only on closer contact with people in the area and careful observation of the community itself that indications of the German heritage of Okarche become evident.

The initial population in Okarche was not predominantly "German" or foreign-born. Indeed, German speakers did not yet numerically dominate the community in 1900, and there were numerous foreign-born of French, Bohemian, Russian, Irish, and English background. Among these the "French" were often German-speakers, and the Irish were closely linked to the German-speaking community through the Catholic Church. A few of the Irish families are still represented in Okarche today. Furthermore, before coming to Okarche, most of the

German-speaking families of the initial population had long-term association with other areas of the United States or Canada. Thus, not only are foreign-born Germans important to the settlement of the town, but first generation German-Americans are prominent as household heads in the 1900 census population.

The German component of the Okarche population is actually more properly distinguished as "Germanic," since it included people from most of central Europe, east European areas which had large German-speaking elements, Denmark, Sweden, Norway, and German-speaking areas of North America which had been established for over a century. Although "standard" German became a primary medium for communication within this population, most of the people spoke different dialects (Willibrand 1950, 1951). Local comments concerning German language used in early Okarche suggest that people could "shut out" large sectors of the population by using more esoteric forms of speech; given the diversity of the

census population, this does not seem to be an unreasonable claim. It is also clear that most families
included bilingual speakers who were competent in
English, especially in the younger generation (manuscript schedules of the Twelfth Census of the United
States suggest that there were very few monolingual
German-speakers).

Numerically more prominent in the initial Okarche
population, although not "dominant" in the sense of
group identity, was a large component of families with
much longer "American" association. These included
farms and a majority of businessmen of the town. The
regions from which these people came were much the same
as the German-speaking population--the settled Midwest
of that day and the northern and western fringes of the
South--although more families in the "Anglo-American"
group were from the New England and Mid-Atlantic regions
than among German-speakers.

The most important characteristics of the early
population in Okarche were its youth and transience.
This is reflected in all of the key records of the
developmental period, including the census materials of
1890 and 1900, tract books noting the homestead claimants of the rural population, newspaper accounts of
events during the first ten to fifteen years after
settlement, Sanborn-Perris maps of the town, church
histories, and individual accounts of early conditions
in the area which are available at present. Indeed, a
very small percentage of the families who participated
in the Okarche district land runs actually remain.

A second wave of migrants to Oklahoma accounts for a
much larger part of the present population base. These
people bought rights to homesteads from original claimants, obtained claims from relatives who had preceded
them into the territory, or filed claims for land which
had been abandoned by original claimants. Thus, continued patterns of migration in and out of the community

and the development of family units in situ are the
demographic factors of greatest importance to the
founding of Okarche.

LOCAL LAND DIVISIONS AND REGIONAL ECONOMIC NETWORKS

The initial tracting of land in the vicinity of
present-day Okarche occurred in two stages. First, the
Oklahoma land run of 1889 created 160-acre homesteads in
the 3,000-square-mile area which had remained unassigned
to Indian groups after the post-Civil War reservation
treaties (see McReynolds 1954). Second, in 1892 the
Cheyenne-Arapaho reservation was opened to settlement,
except those 160-acre lots which, under agreement with
the United States, has been set aside for Indians in
1891 (see Gittinger; McReynolds 1954: 299). The town
of Okarche was established during this later opening,
and is situated only one mile west of the boundary

between the two regions (Map 2). Until 1892, Okarche
settlers of the Oklahoma opening looked to Kingfisher as
their primary place of association. Kingfisher was also
the location of claims offices for both land runs.

The administrative units into which the Okarche
population was divided included Kingfisher County on the
north and Canadian County on the south. The counties
were subdivided into townships, four of which figure
prominently in this study. The Okarche townsite was
tracted on 160 acres of land adjacent to a rail stop and
cattle corrals of the Chicago, Rock Island, and Pacific
Railway. This tract comprised four 40-acre segments of
individual homesteads, two in Harrison township,
Kingfisher County, and two in Rock Island township,
Canadian County (Oklahoma Tract Book). Such claim
duplications were not uncommon during any of the
Oklahoma land openings, although the legal machinery for
dealing with them was improved after the bitter experience of 1889 during which time there was no means of

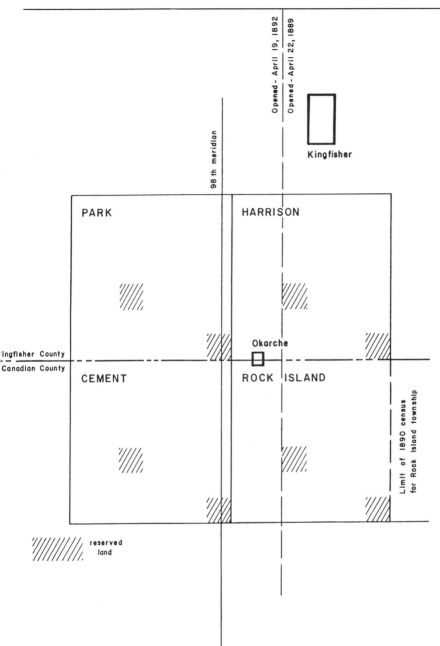

Map 2. Major geographic and political divisions
the Okarche district, and limits of the four-township
nsus sample area.

adjudicating conflicts until eight months after settlement (see McReynolds 1954: 291-292). Thus, the Okarche
townsite was officially certified in two separate court
actions only four months after the April 19th admission
of homesteaders. This placed the town almost at the
intersection of Harrison, Park, Rock Island, and Cement
townships, with its rural population almost evenly
divided among these land divisions.

Selections of this four-township area for the demographic study of early Okarche is based upon documents
which associate people with business transactions and
with the general social resources of the town. That is,
the "Okarche community" is viewed in both a geographic
and social sense--consisting of social networks tied to
economic, political, and religious organizations as well
as their physical manifestations in the town and
surrounding rural area. A particularly helpful information base for this evaluation is a series of public
announcements in mid-1890 local newspapers, which listed

individuals who approach final certification of their homesteads (Okarche Times 1894 and 1895). These notices include the location of property to be certified, the name of its holder, and a list of references who attested that the claimant had indeed satisfied homestead conditions. The personal references are most important since they list names and places of association of several individuals. Thus, they provide not only a record of small personal networks, but a general town identification for each network. By far, the majority of the notices concerning people in the four townships surrounding Okarche center indicate an Okarche identification. However, on the north of Harrison and Park townships, and on the south of Rock Island and Cement townships there are, respectively, numerous references to Kingfisher and El Reno. To the east and west a much more distant indication of association to Okarche is noted, extending out of the four-township zone to a distance of about 8 miles from the center.

In the four-township area surrounding the town then,
a strong but imperfect "identification with Okarche" is
indicated by the documents. In this respect, a second
consideration for demographic study becomes important.
The agricultural census materials of 1900 were both collected and generalized at the township level (Abstract
of the Twelfth Census, 1900, 1902; and Twelfth Census of
the United States: Statistical Atlas, 1903). For this
reason, and considering the rather fortuitous position
of the town within the township matrix, I have limited
detailed demographic consideration to Harrison, Park,
Rock Island, and Cement townships; this allows the use
of general reports on the agricultural census of 1900--a
necessity since the individual agricultural schedules in
Okarche are not available for study. The study area
provides information on perhaps 70 to 80 percent of the
early Okarche service area. Of course, the selected
area also includes a small proportion of families not
strongly associated with Okarche by participation in its

dominant social interactions; but this is to be expected in any areal attempt to delineate social boundaries on the level of "communities."

The community of Okarche is also a product of the broader regional development of north-central Oklahoma, and the economic development of Oklahoma and the nation. North-central Oklahoma is deeply involved today in wheat production, and, to a lesser extent, in natural grass and raw petroleum drilling. The importance of these commodities was felt relatively early after settlement, although none were central to the economy of Okarche until well after the homestead period and Oklahoma statehood. It was a more general interest in the potentials for wheat and other grain production in Oklahoma which provided some of the impetus for individual demands that the area be opened to settlement (see Rister 1942: 201-5; McReynolds 1954: 278-9). As early as 1893, inflated predictions of the wheat yields were printed in area newspapers, together with glowing

estimates of the importance of the region in wheat
farming. However, it is important to note that for most
farmers subsistence, rather than intensive wheat production, was of paramount concern in the earliest years
after settlement.

Unlike cases of initial settlement in several other
areas of the United States, there were few options
available to settlers of Oklahoma as to the location and
arrangement of towns or agricultural land (cf. Jordan
1966; Powell 1963). Of course, most of the people who
moved to Oklahoma from the Midwest were familiar with
the systems used in tracting the territory. However,
changes were undoubtedly felt in the general logistics
of farming activity by almost all of the settlers.
Communications with grain marketing centers, although
they were well established in much of Oklahoma from the
beginning of settlement, were insufficient to allow for
the rapid development of the region's agricultural
potentials. Whereas "towns" might essentially spring up

overnight, farms are a different matter. For most farmers, the 160-acre limitation on government allotments undoubtedly restricted the scale of individual gains in key commodities. Therefore, unless a farmer had reserve resources, it was necessary to pursue a broader, "subsistence oriented" strategy for at least the first few years.

The tract system also predetermined the soil and vegetation composition of homesteads. It was impossible for individuals to maximize balances of soil, cover, and especially water resources, except within the present choices available--when, indeed, there were choices at all. As we shall see, this situation is reflected in the chronology of claims, and migration patterns as new lands were opened in other parts of Oklahoma.

Okarche center was also limited in its initial and developmental functions by the commercial geographic features of Oklahoma Territory. The towns of Kingfisher and El Reno were established three years earlier than

Okarche, and consequently, had served as a logistic base for some rural families who were later closely associated with Okarche. These towns had already developed serve potentials over a wide area, as had Oklahoma City, some 30 miles to the southeast in territorial days. Thus, early business in Okarche was placed in competition with more stable and developed regional competition.

The services offered by the early Okarche center mainly involved construction goods and general supply. There were a few specialty shops--a candy store, a cobbler, and a tin shop--as well as a bank, an insurance corporation, several hotels and saloons, a milling company, a dentist, a barber, and several doctors some of whom were rural land claimants. The history of commercial enterprise in Okarche closely parallels developments in the rural sector of economic activity, particularly with regard to the growth of specialized wheat farming. The supply of essential services and equipment for farming activities was important early, and gained in importance through time. The town has never been a major center for commercial activities over a wide region, although it has recently provided medical services beyond the limits of its business market-zone.

FAMILY, RELIGIOUS AND SOCIAL UNITS

The vast majority of families in the settlement population of Okarche were unrelated nuclear units without long-term prior association with many of their neighbors. However, there were a few constellations of households related through kinship ties at the time of settlement and closely colocated on the land. Almost immediately after the opening of the Cheyenne-Arapaho country and the founding of Okarche, two churches were established which would play an important part in the development of the community. These were St. John's

Lutheran Church and Holy Trinity Catholic Church, the
former with almost a totally German congregation and the
latter with German and Irish parishioners. In addition,
a Congregationalist church was attended mainly by
Anglo-Americans, and a Mennonite Church was founded six
miles south of the center by east-European German-
speakers. There were other congregations--Baptist and
German-Evangelical--but the Catholic, Lutheran, and
Congregational churches have continued into present
times.

The Catholic and Lutheran congregations represent
the most stable social units of Okarche. They continue
to be dominated by families of original homestead period
settlers, each now multiplied into several households
located throughout the Okarche region and in the center.
Some of the factors which have contributed to the
stability of these groups are an early use of German
language (see Willibrand 1950, 1951), programs of
congregation promoted mutual aid, support of regional

church organizations--particulary in the case of the
Lutherans--and the maintenance of separate schools which
has persisted from the period of settlement. This does
not mean that Lutheran and Catholic families have maintained themselves in strong isolation from other
segments of the Okarche population. Rather, the groups
are, and have been since the founding of the town,
strongly identifiable associations which have varied in
composition much less than other church units or more
direct economic and political associations. It is also
in the church groups that German "tradition" is most
evident within the population. Indeed, the religious
patterns practiced by the Okarche congregations contribute the bulk of "cultural elements" which may be
directly and unequivocably identified with the European
backgrounds of the people. In other areas of endeavor,
however, distinctive patterns of activity are not so
clearly apparent.

We must recall that Okarche Germans were involved in
the overall "pioneer" context of adjustive strategies,
risk, and poorly developed logistics. Even the Germans
of early Okarche pursued many different, sometimes
incompatible economic practices under variable land
conditions. Thus successes and failures of many
individuals cannot be attributed in their entirety to
one element of common association, whether it be an
element of heritage, tradition, or corporate action. It
should not be expected that all Germans should have
"succeeded" on the land or in business activities of the
center, regardless of their religious and interpersonal
associations. Indeed, many did not remain in the area
in the long run, even though they were part of the
"traditional" German element of the population; others
remained although they were not of German background.

The families of Okarche today are enmeshed with one
another through long-standing ties of marriage and
cooperation, generally within the three religious

denominations, although with somewhat less force recently than in former years. The patterns of association evident today result from the pioneer building processes which have operated in many other historical and social contexts. These processes include what James Malin (1935) called "turnover," the tendency of a pioneer population to include many "short-term" residents, and what some demographers have called "cumulative inertia," the tendency of a frontier geographic zone to manifest greater and greater levels of population stability through time (Hudson 1977: 18-9). From an individual point of view, households which invest time in a place have a strengthened commitment to remain as that investment grows. Thus, when we view the pioneer population of Okarche, it is not surprising to see a high rate of demographic turnover which is not readily explained by local economic conditions. With the passage of time, however, it is also not surprising to see family continuity and individual persistence,

even in the face of major adverse economic or political
conditions. The understanding of key demographic components of early Okarche history then, incorporates population profiles and family history, both tied to the
contexts of large social associations, economic action,
"ethnic" identifications, and "community" and regional
development. As we shall see in subsequent chapters,
the religious groups centered on "German" ethnic identification are the most important tier of social groups of
this larger system.

CHAPTER III

DEMOGRAPHIC SKETCH OF THE OKARCHE AREA--1889-1940

BACKGROUNDS OF SETTLERS

The settlers of Oklahoma came from practically every part of North America and Europe, but most had strong prior association with the United States. The opening of the Unassigned Lands was accomplished from several starting points, resulting in an initial segregation of people with Midwestern ties on the north, and Southern ties on the south. Okarche is situated in the northern area, and so reflects the Midwestern pattern of states of origin. A number of observational techniques allow the construction of a relatively refined picture of source areas for the Okarche population, as well as a general view of migration patterns prior to the opening of Oklahoma. A simple record of birthplaces for the population provides a starting point in both of these tasks.

Birthplace information for Rock Island and Harrison
townships in 1889 shows that many families had moved
frequently before settling in Oklahoma. In general,
population movement progresses westward, although some
households show return migrations from frontier areas
such as South Dakota and Nebraska, or changes of residence within the upper-Midwest and Appalachia. In one
extreme case, the children of an Indiana couple were
born in Arkansas, Illinois, Texas, Kansas, and Indian
Territory during a fourteen-year period. Another couple
had children in Texas, Kansas, and Colorado during the
ten years prior to their coming to Oklahoma. The
tendency toward migration continued in these cases, for
neither family was present in the Okarche region in
1900. The first gained final certification of a homestead in 1895, but is not in the 1900 census. The
second relinquished a claim by the end of 1890. But the
more typical pattern of births in households shows
longer duration of prior residence in states of the

Midwest and the central prairies, with successions of several births for one or two places.

The birthplace record of the 1889 population enumerated in the 1890 census (Table 1) readily displays the relative contribution of each source area, and suggests some qualitative differences in the significance of several "key" states to Oklahoma settlement. A total of 135 (61%) of the over-20 individuals born in the United States were from Missouri, Illinois, Kentucky, Indiana, and Ohio. The relative distance of these states from Oklahoma is reflected in the under-20 births, providing one strong indication of the chronology of westward movement during the years preceding the Oklahoma openings. The addition of people from Iowa, Tennessee, Pennsylvania, and Kansas accounts for 188 (85%) of the over-20 population. With the exception of Kansas, these states show moderate numbers of under-20 individuals. The very high number of Kansas births is the result of the pre-opening activities in that state immediately

	Primary Place of association before 1889 (households)a	Households reporting births	Total Births	Births of persons under 20 in 1889	Births of persons over 20 in 1889
Kansas	16	35	90	78	12
Missouri	9	29	57	24	33
Illinois	8	28	49	20	29
Kentucky	5	16	35	13	22
Indiana	2	21	29	4	25
Ohio	1	21	27	1	26
Iowa	3	17	25	9	16
Tennessee	2	10	21	7	14
Pennsylvania	2	7	20	9	11
Texas	4	5	9	9	0
Wisconsin	1	5	5	0	5
Virginia	1	3	7	0	7
Michigan	1	2	4	2	2
Nebraska	1	2	4	4	0
South Dakota	1	1	4	4	0
Southb	0	9	9	2	7
Northeastb	0	12	12	0	12
Westb	0	6	7	7	0

a. Any household reflecting long-term residence in a state is included in this count. Long-term residence was determined through place-of-birth information on children. Conjugal households in which all members (Father, Mother, first child) show the same birthplace are included also.

b. South includes Alabama, Arkansas, Mississippi, Georgia and North Carolina; Northeast includes New York, Maryland, Connecticut and Maine; West includes Colorado, No Man's Land, and Indian Territory.

Table 1. Places of Origin of the 1889 population of Rock Island and Harrison townships, including persons in foreign-born-headed households (Compiled from the manuscript schedules of the Oklahoma Territorial Census of 1890).

prior to 1889, although 16 of 144 households in the 1890
territorial census had long prior association with
Kansas. Thus, Kansas, Missouri, Illinois, and Kentucky
account for 135 (70%) of the under-20 population in
1890, and the addition of Iowa, Tennessee, Pennsylvania,
and Texas brings the total of 169 (87%).

Another way of estimating the significance of the
contribution of each source state to Okarche settlement
is by observing the duration of residence by households.
This is the purpose of the "primary place" column of
Table 1. Households showing successive births of
children in one state, or births of all family members
(regardless of household size) in a state, were counted
as having a primary association to the place involved.
Of course, single individuals and couples were deleted
from this listing, leaving only conjugal family units
and extended family households. While the criteria for
considering a household to have had prior strong ties
with a place are somewhat subjective, the resulting

associations augment the information form birthplace counts in two ways. First, the general pattern of primary contributing states is refined to place less emphasis on certain places showing large numbers of births, such as Indiana and Ohio. Similarly, Texas shows a low number of total births but four family associations, and so requires more emphasis. Second, with the exceptions of Wisconsin, Virginia, Michigan, Nebraska, and South Dakota, no other places provide indications of long-term association. Therefore, a large number of states and territories which occur as birthplaces listed for the early Okarche population are deleted from further consideration, since they relate only to individuals of the population or to very short terms of residence.

From these data, we see that the older population of the 1889 run in the Okarche area had its roots in the Midwest primarily, and that most families had considerable first-hand pioneer and settled experience with farming communities in the prairie-woodland belt of Illinois, Iowa, Missouri, and Kansas. However, a relatively small number of households from Kentucky, Tennessee, and Pennsylvania account for a rather large number of the settlers--about 18% of the population. The census materials confirm that several large families from these areas included older parents and nearly adult children. Other states-of-origin made their contribution more in "births" than in "experience." The most significance departure from this rule involves those households with foreign-born heads.

Table 2 depicts the places of birth and immigration chronology of the foreign-born individuals in the early Okarche population. These figures are not to be taken as indicative of "ethnic groups" per se because there were also first-generation European-American household heads who are not adequately reflected in the 1890 census materials. The seven source countries in 1889 were dominated by Germany, England, and (English)

A. Place of Birth — Age in five-year cohorts

Place of Birth	Number of Households	10-14	15-19	20-24	25-29	30-34	35-39	40-44	45-49	50-54	55-59	60-64
Bohemia	1	1	1						1		1	
Canada	5				1	1	1	1		1		1
England	4			1		2				1		
Germany	9			1	5	2	1	1			2	1
Ireland	2	1							2	1	1	
Russia	2			1		1						
Sweden	2				3							
TOTALS	25	2	1	3	9	6	2	2	3	3	4	2

B. Place of Birth — Total amount of time in United States in five-year intervals[a]

Place of Birth	0-4	5-9	10-14	15-19	20-24	25-29	30-34	35-39	40-44	45-49	50-54
Canada	1					3	1	1			
England		1	1	2			1				
Germany		3	5	2	1			1	1	1	1
Ireland					2				1	1	1
Russia			1			1					
Sweden			1		1						
TOTALS	1	4	8	4	4	4	2	2	2	2	2

a. Not reported for all individuals by census takers.

Table 2. Foreign-born persons in the 1890 Census of Rock Island and Harrison townships, depicting (A) place of birth by age groups and (B) years residence in the U.S. before 1890 (Compiled from the manuscript schedules of the Oklahoma Territorial Census of 1890).

Canada. Most of the population was over 20 years old, and 83% of those individuals for which immigration dates are reported in the census had ten years or more experience in the United States. This acquaintance with America follows the internal locational patterns of settlers born in the United States, except that Kentucky and Tennessee account for none of the foreign-born families.

The 1900 census materials augment this general picture, but also provide some striking contrasts between the populations which initially entered the Unassigned lands and the Cheyenne-Arapaho reservation. Figure 1 presents age-sex and marital information for the population of Cement township in 1900, organized according to place of birth. Kentucky, Ohio, Indiana, and Illinois are represented predominantly by individuals over 20 years of age, while Missouri, Kansas, and Nebraska reflect births mainly between the years 1880 and 1900. The foreign-born of this population are

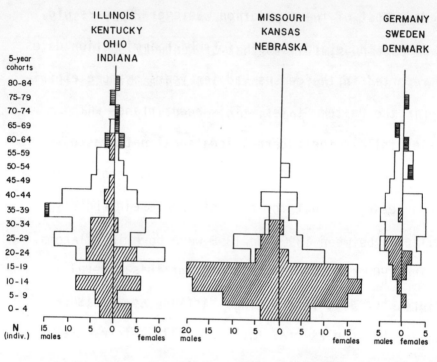

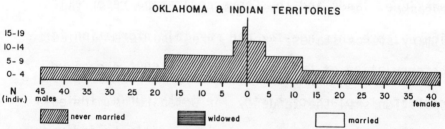

Figure 1. Age-sex profiles of the 1900 population of Cement township showing major contributing states differentiated by their location in the migration field (low frequency places omitted; compiled from manuscript schedules of the 1900 census).

considerably more numerous than in 1889. They display an age pattern similar to that of Kentucky, Ohio, Indiana, and Illinois. Finally, Oklahoma births fill out the base of the population, especially in the 0-4 cohort. These profiles also show the continued immigration which occurred during the early years of settlement. Fewer than half of the children born into this population between 1890 and 1895 were born in Oklahoma.

The frontier marriage pattern reflected in these materials is also interesting. A large number of the youngest married females came from Missouri, Kansas, and Nebraska. These women were married to men from the primary source states, except three who were married to men from Germany. All sectors of the Cement township population show the tendency for women to be married between the ages of 20 through 24, and for men to remain single longer. Indeed, the early marriage ages for women fall in the late teens, while the men they begin in the early twenties. But the marriage-age spans for women and men end at 25 and 35 respectively.

The apparent difference in the marriage age of men
in the American-born and European-born sectors of the
Cement township population is the result of small
population size. This difference is not strongly
reflected in he total population of the region. There
is a difference, however, in the sexual balance of the
two groups. There were relatively few European-born
single males who came to the Okarche region, other than
those attached to the households of their parents.
Further, of the 22 married men form Germany, Sweden, and
Denmark in Cement township in the 1900, only one married
a woman born in the United States to American-born
parents. The others all married women of European background, and only two of those women were born in the
United States. Yet only seven of the marriages took
place in Europe, so approximately two-thirds of these
men came to North America as single males. Similarly,
all but two of the married women born in Germany,
Sweden, and Denmark from this population were married to

European-born men. Most of the women came to the United
States as children, while several of the men came as
adults. Thus, among those individuals who entered the
United States as single persons, a pattern of marriage
practice similar to non-Germans in its locational
aspects is represented, although selection on the basis
of heritage seems to be strongly manifested. The women
were in North America, and in some cases, the frontier
areas of the continent, prior to the arrival of the men
they would marry. Finally, there is a total of 13
married men of German heritage reflected in the
American-born age-sex profiles of Figure 1. These men
also married women of similar background--primarily
other German-Americans.

Thus, the German-American component of the early
Okarche community reflects strong commonality of heritage throughout its adult population, but a range of
American migration and settlement experience is no less
broader than the population of the region in general.

Indeed, at no time during the settlement period of
Okarche do we encounter a large proportion of recent
migrants from Europe or large groups entering the region
from any one place in the United States.

The pattern of source states differs slightly
between the 1889 and 1892 settlement areas, at least as
reflected by 1900 census data for the Cheyenne-Arapaho
area. Nebraska, for example, is of much greater importance in the later run, while Pennsylvania and Tennessee
are of much less significance. Nebraska accounts for 32
births within the Cement township population, but
Pennsylvania and Tennessee together were the birthplaces
of only 16 individuals, five of whom were under ten
years of age. Furthermore, the Nebraska-born individuals are predominantly unmarried teens, representing
several prior long-term resident families from more
northern prairie farm communities. Iowa remains prominent as a source of Okarche population, but ambiguous
from the point of view of age. Many other states are

represented by one to five individuals, and had little real impact on the composition of the population during either land run.

The foreign-born of Cement township also included a single male from Spain, a married woman from France and a couple from French Canada. There were no Czechs in the township, but representatives of all of the other European countries which were present in the 1889 run are found in the Cement township census.

The differences in the backgrounds of people in the 1889 and 1892 settlement areas of Okarche result from national economic conditions and the processes of communication between initial settlers and friends of like background in other parts of the United States. For example, as Willibrand (1951: 285) has pointed out, at least one German individual who established himself during the Oklahoma run carried on correspondence with people to the east and north which was aimed at brining more Germans in Okarche. Moreover, population pressure

in some of the more settled areas of the east--
especially as coupled with the aura of opportunity
presented in newspaper treatments of Oklahoma--provided
impetus for individual attempts to settle well into the
Twentieth Century. The "push" factors were a combination of rising land prices and a settled mature population in areas such as Illinois, Iowa, Indiana, Missouri,
and even Kansas and Nebraska, both of which made it
difficult for young couples to establish new farms or
for established farmers to increase their holdings. The
"pull" factors were relatively inexpensive land amenable
to rapid improvement, excellent initial logistic support
in the form of railroads and a large commercial population, and a comparatively stable political situation.
But we should suspect, given major differences in the
source states responsible for the base populations of
different land openings, that the "push" factors were
more important in determining who arrived in Oklahoma
for settlement.

HOUSEHOLD COMPOSITION AND AGE-SEX STRUCTURE

The overwhelming majority of households during the
settlement period of Okarche consisted of conjugal
family units (throughout this discussion the terminology
of Hammel and Laslett 1974, as modified by Kertzer 1977,
is employed). Most of these households were unrelated
to other settlers of the immediate locality, although a
few kin networks established themselves on adjacent or
very nearly adjacent homesteads. Figure 2 depicts the
household composition and kinship relations of all such
networks recorded in the 1908 census and reflected in
the Oklahoma Tract Book. Four of these extended kin
networks (Figure 2, a-d) represent sets of brothers,
while two consist of father-son pairs (Figure 2, e and
f). There were only two extended family households in
the 1900 census. One (Figure 2, g) was the three-
generation household of an old couple. The other
included a man in his sixties accompanied by a

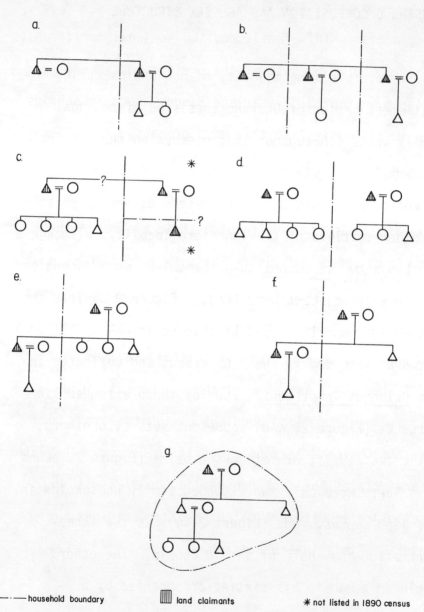

Figure 2. Household composition and kin relations of family networks in the 1890 population of Harrison and Rock Island townships (compiled from manuscript schedule of the 1890 Oklahoma census).

33-year-old wife, four sons ranging in age from 27-34, and grandson. This family and two conjugal family units are interesting because of the presence of several children in the 25-35 year age range. Such households look suspiciously like they were preparing for later land openings, and indeed only one of these families remained through 1900. However, the two families that left Okarche did not relinquish their claims in the Unassigned Lands area until the very late 1890's, and so they evidently did not capitalize on the opportunities of the Cheyenne-Arapaho and Cherokee Strip openings. Other households consisted of several siblings in their middle twenties, and some of these apparently did "stage" for later land openings by taking a poor claim near the Cheyenne-Arapaho reservation border. The late date of claims for such households, coupled with the dates of relinquishment matching other openings, lends support to this interpretation.

An age-sex profile of the 1889 population of Rock Island and Harrison townships is presented in Figure 3. It is apparent form this profile that the general settler population was young, as might be expected in a case with a large predominance of conjugal family units. The sex ratio for the 1889 settlers was 134:100, reflecting many unmarried males between the ages of 20 and 40. Very few of the men under 25 were married, and half of the 25-29 cohort was single. Most of the women over 20 were married, however, as well as half of the women in the 15-19 cohort. This age-sex pattern is typical of frontier situations which have been investigated by others (Lefferts 1977), including the constriction of the profile into an "hourglass" form. The constriction involves the 15-19 cohort in the 1889 population, indicating that most couples were in the early years of childbearing. This means that the potential for population growth through births was great immediately after settlement, the potential for work

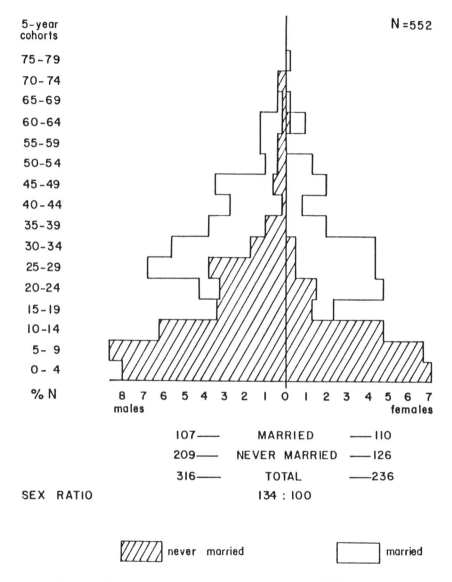

Figure 3. Age-sex profile of the 1889 population of Rock Island and Harrison townships (compiled from manuscript schedules of the 1890 Oklahoma census).

output on homesteads would remain high during the first
10 to 15 years, and pressure on the land through new
marriages and births stemming from the under-20 cohorts
would be deferred over at least the same period of time.

The people included in Figure 3 number 552 individuals, representing 155 households located in a 48
square mile area. In addition to the two extended
family households noted above, there were 72 conjugal
family units, 19 married couples with no children, and
51 single individuals. Only two single land claimants
were women, and there were very few households listed in
the 1890 census but not in the Oklahoma Tract Book. The
families without land all left the Okarche region before
1900. Among the homesteaders the potentials for satis-
fying claim conditions differed greatly from household
to household. This is strongly reflected in the demographic picture gained from study of the original
settler families remaining in Okarche through 1900. In
the first ten years after settlement, 377 of the

original 552 people in the 1890 census either left the community or died. Most left, leaving only 50 of the original households and one newly married couple who established an independent farm close to the man's parent's homestead. Only seven of the single male claimants, one widow, and six of the married couples present in 1890 remained in 1900. The other successful eighty-niners were initially larger family units. Thus, 42% of the families with children remained on their homesteads through the first ten years, while only 31% of the couples and 15% of the single persons remained over the same timespan.

The dynamics of household composition and basic population features for the 50 households present in both 1890 and 1900 are complex. Using an abbreviated classification of households which reflects age, sex, and generational distinctions, it is possible to view the changing patterns of family composition for the purposes of assessing work potentials on homesteads.

Figure 4 presents a count of households in each class
for the two census years, and a flow diagram indicating
household class changes which occurred over the ten year
period. The diagram shows that even though the figures
for most of the household classes are similar in the two
years, the actual households in each class are generally
different. Thus, although there were 15 couples with at
least one child over ten years of age in the 1890 household breakdown, the 17 similar households in 1900
included only nine of the same families. In this fixed
household sample, we could expect the number of such
households to be reduced over a subsequent ten-year
period, and for major increases to occur in the formation of extended family households or couples with all
children over ten years of age. In a broader view of
Okarche population, the turnover in households would
introduce new families in classes B, C, and D, which
would also go through a process of compositional change
leading to household extension or maturity, depending
upon continued conditions of land availability.

Household Class	1890	1900
A. Single Male	7	2
B. Couple	4	1
C. Couple with children 0-9	12	8
D. Couple with at least one child over 10	15	17
E. Couple with all children over 10	4	5
F. Old Couple	2	5
G. Widow(er) living alone	1	1
H. Extended Family Household	1	7
I. Female head of household	2	4
J. Household with attached unrelated persons	2	3
Total Households:	50	51

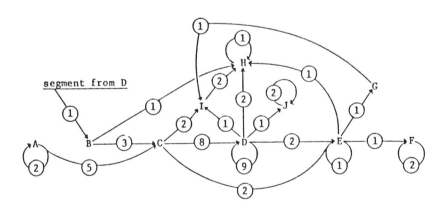

Figure 4. Comparison of household structures in 1890 and 1900 for 50 settler households remaining in Okarche over the first ten years of settlement, including frequency of household class changes (compiled from manuscript schedules of the Oklahoma Territorial Census of 1890 and the U.S. Census of 1900).

The changes in household class of the settler population which remained from 1890 through 1900 reflects, then, an incomplete picture of a large family cycle, and the data underscore the relative youth of the families involved. Even as the most "mature" households of Okarche in 1900, the initial claimant population still mainly involved parents who were only in the middle of their childbearing years. This is true of extended family households and households which included attached unrelated persons. Indeed, only two of the extended family households of 1900 included elderly male heads who were initial land claimants (Figure 5, a and b). A third household of the same class (Figure 5c) included a male head 45 years old and three sons over age 20, one of whom was married and had a child. The remaining complex households include several different situations centered on female family heads or the attachment of elderly lineal or young collateral relatives. Thus, one extended family (Figure 5d) resulted

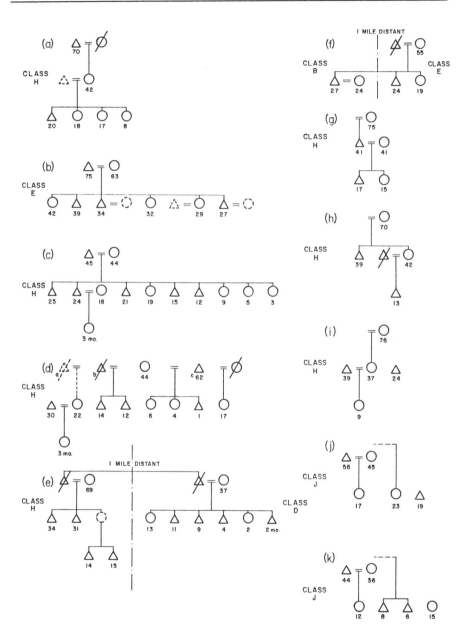

Figure 5. Complex households in the 1900 census sample (compiled from the manuscript schedules of the 1900 census).

from the marriage of a woman claimant paired with the
marriage of her daughter, and the remaining complex
households included a network of widowed sisters-in-law
(Figure 5e), a mother-son two-household network (Figure
5f), and three households which included mothers of
primary individuals (Figure 5, g through i). Two households added unrelated individuals and nephews or nieces
(Figure 5, g and k). In none of these cases is there
reason to believe that the impetus for family extension
was based on inheritance; nor is there a "pattern" of
household extension indicated by the data.

While the conditions on the Oklahoma frontier seem
to have favored larger conjugal family units and complex
households, at least during the first ten years, younger
couples probably found it easier to establish themselves
as farming and commerce in the area stabilized. It
should be emphasized that although turnover of the
Okarche population was great during the first few years
after settlement, it dropped radically before 1900.

Thus, an age difference of 15 to 20 years separated the older children of the diverse households in 1900, with the great majority of these children being under age 20. For this reason, as well as because of the competition for available homesteads immediately after 1900, a more complete family cycle would show a number of extended family households including children in their twenties between 1900 and 1915. The agricultural system favored concentration of family labor resources on initial homesteads coupled with additional land acquired through purchase by initial land claimants. There were few new farms established by young couples during the same period then, either from the outside or by children of homesteaders. The age structure and turnover features of the older Okarche population, furthermore, set the span of the initial generational land turnover at about ten years, beginning in about 1915 and lasting through 1925. During this period original homesteads and additional farmland acquired in the name of the settlers

were either pre-inherited by a child or divided among
several children, the actual disposition depending upon
the amount of land available for transfer.

A number of other characteristics of the initial
settler population which remained in the Okarche area
through 1900 elucidate factors which mediated success on
the Oklahoma farming frontier. The sex ratio of the
successful households was slightly lower than that of
the general population of 1890, for example, and it
balanced from 115:100 in 1890 to 109:100 in 1900. This
reflects the reduced number of single males who represented a prominent part of the total 1890 population.
The change in size and sex ratio of the population is
the cumulative result of births, deaths, migrations, and
marriage. During the ten year period following settlement, the following changes in the composition of the
population are reflected by census records: 89 recorded
births, 9 recorded deaths, 29 lost through either
unrecorded death or migration, 9 additions through

marriage, and 25 additions through migration of relatives. These changes brought a net increase of 85
people, from 213 persons to 298. The impact of these
changes on the age-sex structure of the combined households is shown in Figure 6. In addition to greater
sexual balance, the age-sex pyramids show an increase in
the combined work potential of the households. The
large full-time productive sector of the population
(persons from 15 to 59) had increased from 112 to 161
people (from 52.5% to 54.0%). Thus, there was not only
an increase on a per capita basis, but also a slight
increase in the proportion of working-age householders
to less-productive members of the population. Meanwhile, the under-15 cohorts increased from 97 to 120
individuals, but dropped on a percentage basis from
45.5% to 40.2% of all people on these farms. This
decrease was matched by an increase in the over-59
cohorts from a total of four individuals in 1890 to 17
in 1900, or 1.8% of the population to 5.7%,
respectively.

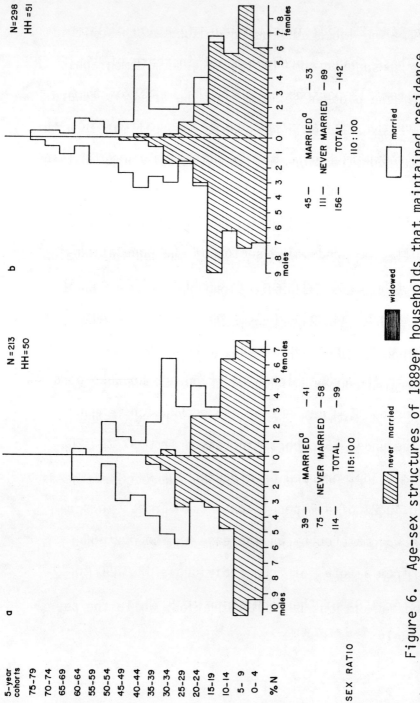

Figure 6. Age-sex structures of 1889er households that maintained residence in the Okarche area through 1900 for the years 1890 and 1900 (compiled from manuscript schedules of the 1890 Oklahoma census and the 1900 census).

By viewing isolated households such as these it is possible to suggest some of the long-term demographic trends of the pioneer settlement. One trend is toward an older, sexually balanced population, ultimately with no radical constrictions in its pyramidal form. But in the ongoing settlement process the continued in- and out-flow of households contributed to the youth of the settler community. Turnover, then, impeded the development of an age-sex structure along the lines of what might have been projected from the patterns of the settler population at any given time. The decision of a young married couple to locate in the same area as their parents, in a totally new area, or with one of the parents in an extended household situation, was generally mediated by land availability and the economic needs of all concerned. Thus, for a time, the new youth which did enter the settlement came from more established agricultural areas where land and economic conditions afforded few options but out-migration, while the peer

group of these new arrivals already on the Oklahoma
frontier remained attached to their parents while building an interest in an inheritable capital estate. This
whole process constituted what is properly called the
"adjustive" phase of settlement. Its end was marked by
the generational transition from settler parents to
their children and the close of entry into the region by
families from outside the Oklahoma frontier, both of
which occurred during World War I. After the adjustive
phase the tendency of the population toward a less
youthful age distribution and more balanced sex ratios
proceeded without impeding effects, and a regular
pyramidal age structure was established.

TURNOVER, DEMOGRAPHIC STRUCTURE, AND SETTLER BACKGROUND

The chronology of claims and transfers of claim in the Okarche region indicates the rate of turnover for each of the two settlement areas. Table 3 summarizes the claims and household replacements for part of the Unassigned Lands and Cheyenne-Arapaho Reservation, and shows a number of differences in the patterns of change in population for the two areas. The data refer to: (1) all of the Unassigned Lands homesteads in the study area, a block four miles wide and twelve miles long on the east edge of Harrison and Rock Island townships, and (2) the two-mile wide strip of the same townships settled in 1892. The settlement of the Unassigned Lands near Okarche was not complete by the end of 1889. A total of 21 initial claims came after 1889, one as late as 1892. On the other hand, the settlement of the Cheyenne-Arapaho tracts in the Okarche area was virtually complete within a month of the land opening. The two

Year	Cheyenne-Arapaho Lands					
	New Claims	Claim Replacements	Household Total	New Claims	Claim Replacements	Household Total
1889				165	8 (5%)[a]	165
1890				16 (10%)[b]	36 (20%)	181
1891				4 (2%)	18 (10%)	185
1892	94	27 (28%)[a]	94	1 (.5%)	16 (9%)	186
1893	1	25 (26%)	95		6 (3%)	186
1894	1	5 (5%)	96		2 (1%)	186
1895		3 (3%)	96		1 (.5%)	186
1896		1 (1%)	96			
1897		2 (2%)	96			
1898		1 (1%)	96			

a. N divided by total of same year
b. N divided by total of previous year

Table 3. New claims and turnover rates for Rock Island and Harrison townships from 1889 through 1898 (compiled from the complete record of claims in Rock Island and Harrison townships in the Oklahoma Tract Book).

areas also differed in the rate of replacement during the first year of settlement and in the overall pattern of replacement until relatively stable conditions were established. In the 1889 area, only eight homesteads were relinquished to new claimants during the first year, representing a figure of 5% replacement. However, in the 1892 area 27 homesteads changed hands over a similar length of time. This figure involves 28% of the available tracts in the part of the Cheyenne-Arapaho area considered. Moreover, the replacements in the Unassigned Lands area never exceeded 20% in any given year subsequent to settlement, while turnover in the Cheyenne-Arapaho area remained high through 1893.

These differences relate in part to the proximity of Okarche to the starting points of the two land runs. The lands nearest the edges of the areas opened were taken quickly, accounting for the rapid claim saturation in 1892. The staring points for the Oklahoma run were distant from the Okarche region, so a few tracts

remained untaken for several months. The availability
of land and town-based opportunities ties probably
accounts for the differences in turnover rates over the
first few years. The Unassigned Lands section of the
Okarche rural sector experienced most of its critical
adjustment during the years prior to the founding of the
commercial center. The later settlers could more easily
seek an alternative claim in the west, or leave farming
entirely to attempt the establishment of a business in
the center. There was also a high rate of turnover on
claims in the four quarter-sections which surrounded the
town, and adjacent to Indian allotments to the north of
the center.

It is easily seen that both areas of settlement in
the Okarche region experienced high rates of turnover
during the first few years after homesteading, and that
the entire region was relatively stable by 1895. Yet
the three year difference in starting points and the
turnover variations of the two areas are reflected in

the age-sex structures of the 1900 population. For

example, if we compare an age-sex pyramid for the entire

population of Cement township (Figure 7) to that of the

households of initial Unassigned Lands claimants (Figure

6, b), both populations considered as of 1900, there is

a five-year disparity in the overall age structures

observed. The 1900 Cement township profile is more

similar to that of the 1889ers in 1890 (Figures 3 and 6,

a). The same is true of German population of Cement and

Park townships which compared to the Germans of Rock

Island and Harrison townships (Figure 8). The profile

of the areas dominated by earlier settlers shows a large

40-44 cohort, constriction at the 20-24 cohort, and the

beginnings of a decline in births manifested as a

constriction of the 0-4 cohorts. That of the townships

fully in the Cheyenne-Arapaho area reflects a younger

adult sector, a small 15-19 cohort, and a large 0-4

base.

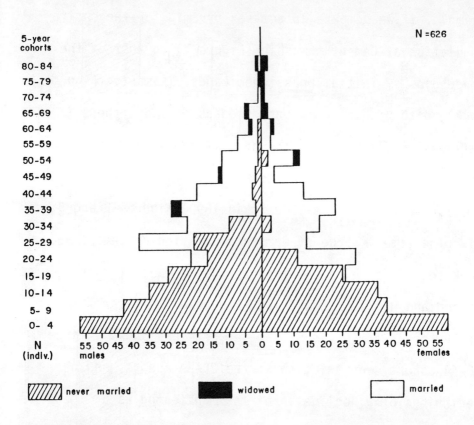

Figure 7. Age-Sex profile of Cement Township in 1900 (compiled from the manuscript schedules of the 1900 census).

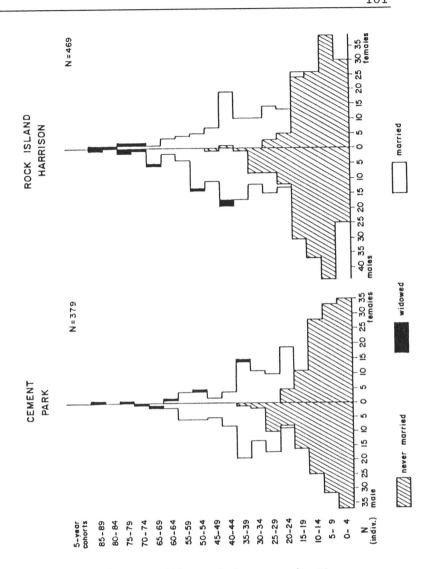

Figure 8. Age-Sex profiles of Germans in the
Oklahoma Run area (Rock Island and Harrison townships)
and Cheyenne-Arapaho Run area (Cement and park townships)
in 1900 (compiled from manuscripts schedules of the
1900 census).

A more important consequence of the sequence of settlement in the Okarche region was the production of variable patterns of household organization through time. This variation is also expressed in differences between the areas settled in 1889 and 1892, as well as in a clearly differentiated town pattern. In discussion above, some of the dynamics of household change in successful families of 1889 were introduced, based on data summarized in Figure 4. By observing the different household patterns in the two settlement areas and the town, it is possible to construct a general picture of household dynamics of the settlement era. Table 4 presents the simple classification of household types for all of Cement and Rock Island townships and for Okarche Center, as of 1900. Since both the town and Cement township were settled in 1892, it is not surprising that they reflect many similarities. However, they also reflect differences stemming from the distinctive makeup of rural and town population, so in some respects

Cement township is more similar to Rock Island township
than to the town. In all three areas a distinction has
been made between "German" and "non-German" population.

These data show that household organization, like
age-sex structure, follows similar patterns for Germans
and non-Germans in the Okarche region. Thus, the most
frequent household class for both groups in Cement township in 1900 was "couples with children 0-9 years of
age." But in Rock Island township more households of
both groups had children over 10 years of age. If there
is any overall difference in German and non-German
segments of the population, it is that German families
on the older end of family development cycles (in
classes E, F, and H of Table 4) are slightly less
frequent than the non-German families. However, in
their basic characteristics, the household development
cycles of the Germans are the same as for the population
as a whole. There is no indication that family organization on the household level conferred any special

advantage to Germans, particularly in the area of economic potentials in the homestead situation.

The frequency of "single male" households in Cement township does not appear to be consistent with the observation made for the 1889 area that single farmers seemed to be at a disadvantage. Inspection of the census lists show that only one of the single males in Cement township was engaged in a non-agricultural occupation. Eight of the remaining single males were land claimants, and the other eleven were employed as farm labor. Therefore, the "success" rate of single claimants is probably actually in line with that deve- lopment where dual-census inspection was possible. The most typical household association of single males in Okarche during this period was as a "boarder." There are therefore many single individuals in both areas not directly listed as "households" but indicated in the census as attached members of larger households.

There is also a larger percentage of extended family households in Cement township than in Rock Island township as of 1900. This is evidently the result of a greater tendency to attach mothers, fathers, and siblings to households than was observed in settlers of the 1889 land run. Such attachment is not surprising in a settlement situation where logistics were more well established. It should be remembered that there was only one extended family household among the 50 initial claimant families who remained in Harrison and Rock Island townships during the first 10 years of Okarche's development, and that only six such households were formed during the first 10 years.

The frequencies of both single male and extended family households are similar for Cement township and Okarche Center. In time, however, one would expect to see greater similarities in both classes of household between the two rural population components. Based upon the isolated household information summarized in Figure

4, the expectation for single males would involve continued reductions through marriage and migrations out of the Okarche area. Conversely, also as indicated above, extended family households would be expected to increase in number throughout the rural territories. In addition, the nature of extended families would be expected to change, resulting in a lower frequency of sibling-pairs and a higher frequency of three-generation patricentric households. Meanwhile, the town would be expected to at least maintain its complement of single males and reflect fewer cases of household extension.

These short-term projections are consistent with known later conditions in Okarche, particularly as regards the German population. The town remained essentially "non-German" much longer than the rural areas surrounding it, while initial German families added to their holdings and provided a "pull" effect on people of similar background. Families matured on the land, adding to their overall work potential, and ultimately contributed older population to the town as some farmers retired to Okarche. Therefore, beginning in the late 1920's and early 1930's, the age structure of the center began to shift dramatically. Until then it had remained a center dominated by the youngest segments of the region's population--it would eventually become dominated by the oldest, the retired settlers leaving farm work for the younger generations.

The town was also dominated by females in the under-20 cohorts. Indeed, the overall sex ratio of the center was 92:100 in 1900, even though males over 20 years of age outnumbered females (see Figure 9). One explanation of this disparity from the normal male-dominated population of the region during the settlement period is to be found in the small population size of Okarche center. The census reflects 319 individuals, 166 of whom were women. Among middle-aged households-- those with children in their teens--the sex balance is disrupted by the loss of male children to work elsewhere

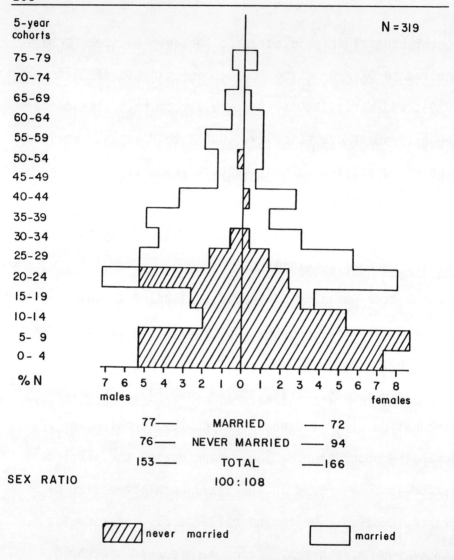

Figure 9. Age-sex profile of Okarche Center in 1900 (compiled from the manuscript schedules of the 1900 census).

or independent settlement opportunities. In the younger families, however, there were apparently many more female births. A check of the census for household classes C and D shows a full accounting of children reported as born to most mothers. Among these households are several with all female children. In such a small population, it does not take too many sexually imbalanced households--such as that of the hotel keeper with seven daughters ranging in age from 5 to 18--to produce radically skewed sex proportions in 5-year cohorts.

Household classes (Table 4) and age-sex data (Figure 9) both serve to strongly differentiate the town of Okarche during its early years from the farming population it served. The center had the highest frequencies of single males and young couples without children and an absolute predominance of households with children under ten years of age (31.4%). The average household size in the center in 1900 was four persons, while that

Household Class	Cement Township German	Other	Total	Okarche Center(a) German	Other	Total	Rock Island Township German	Other	Total
A. Single Male	3	17	20 (15.0%)	3	13	16 (17.9%)	3	6	9 (5.6%)
B. Young Couple	1	2	3 (2.2%)	4	7	11 (12.3%)	5	9	14 (8.7%)
C. Couple with children 0-9	16	22	38 (28.5%)	5	23	28 (31.4%)	10	20	30 (18.8%)
D. Couple with at least one child over 10	14	16	30 (22.6%)	1	10	11 (12.3%)	14	44	58 (36.2%)
E. Couple with all children	4	10	14 (10.5%)	1	8	9 (10.1%)	6	25	31 (19.4%)
F. Old Couple		6	6 (4.5%)		2	2 (2.2%)	1	4	5 (3.1%)
G. Widow(er) living alone		1	1 (.7%)		2	2 (2.2%)		2	2 (1.2%)
H. Extended Family Households	4	17	21 (15.8%)	3	7	10 (11.2%)	3	8	11 (6.8%)
Total Households			133			89			160

	Cement Township German	Other	Okarche Center German	Other	Rock Island Township German	Other
Classes of Households with female heads--frequency	C-1, E-2	E-2		E-1		D-1, E-3
Classes of Households with unrelated attached persons included--frequency	B-1, C-3, D-2	C-1, D-1, E-2, F-1, H-3	C-1, H-1	C-3, D-2, E-1, H-2	B-1, C-2, D-1, E-1	B-1, C-3, D-4, E-3, G-1, H-3

(a) Includes population of center in both Rock Island and Harrison townships.

Table 4. Household classes of Cement and Rock-Island townships, and of Okarche Center in 1900, differentiated by background (compiled from the manuscript schedules of the Twelfth Census of the United States, 1900).

of Cement township was five persons. The center also
had the highest number of married people relative to
total population. The married couples and elderly
individuals in widowed status comprised 46.8% of persons
residing in the town, a far greater proprotion than the
32.9% component of married people among the 1889
settlers. The German population of the town and all
four surrounding townships consisted of 63.1% unmarried
persons, 3% widows, and 33.9% married persons.

These comparisons underscore the particularly fluid
nature of the town population in early Okarche--a fluidity which is probably typical of most centers during the
early years of Oklahoma settlement. If farming a homestead was a tenuous undertaking, then starting a
business amidst the uncertainties of the agricultural
sector was even more tenuous. Several businesses in
Okarche captured local clientele, but established towns
such as Kingfisher and El Reno shaved the service area
in which serious competition could be mustered. The

size of the German population rapidly became a factor of
importance to businessmen, since losing German customers
could make the difference between success or failure.
In addition, much of the local trade with farmers in the
early years was carried out on a barter basis, or
involved extention of credit. These factors contributed
to continued turnover among townbased entrepreneur
families through the early 1900's. The availability of
limited day-labor and clerks positions also kept the
proportion of young and single households relatively
high.

The most important consequence of the turnover
period, however, was the establishment in the Okarche
region of German families in the rural areas primarily
to the west of town, but also on the east in the
Oklahoma land run area. Figure 10 shows the backgrounds
of settlers in Harrison and Rock Island townships by
national groups between the years 1889 and 1895. In
1889 (Figure 10 a) there were only nine households

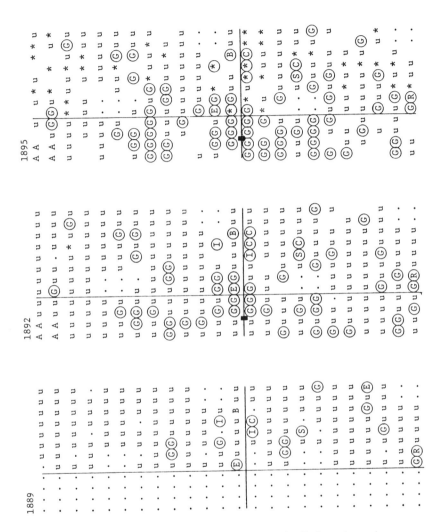

Figure 10. Claims sequence for Rock Island and Harrison townships by place of origin from 1889 through 1895 (A = Cheyenne-Arapaho, B = Bohemia, C = Canada, E = England, G = Germany, I = Ireland, u = United States, R = Russia (compiled from the Oklahoma Trace Book and the manuscript schedules of the 1890 Oklahoma census and the 1900 census).

comprised of German immigrants or first-generation
German Americans. It is clear from the increase of
Germans in 1892 (Figure 10 b) that much of the impetus
for concentration of people from Germany, Sweden,
Denmark, Austria, and Switzerland around Okarche
occurred with the Cheyenne-Arapaho run. On the 1889
side of the land run boundary, the number of German
households had increased to 20 by 1892. Some of these
households came before the 1892 run as part of the
flurry of transfers of 1890 and 1891. Many, however,
took relinquished claims at the same time that the other
area was opened for settlement. Meanwhile, a total of
24 initial claims were established by people of German
background in the part of the Cheyenne-Arapaho territory
immediately west of the starting line, in Rock Island
and Harrison townships. A great many other households
established themselves in Cement and Park townships.

But the German entry into the region did not stop
immediately. Four additional households established

themselves in Harrison and Rock Island townships east of
the land run boundary, and 19 households took advantage
of the turnover conditions west of the line between 1892
and 1895 (Figure 10 c). During the same period, a total
of seven German households left farms located in the two
townships. Thus, the total German component of the
eastern townships of the Okarche region rose from 44 to
60 households by 1895. By 1900 there were 167 households with foreign-born or first-generation "German"
affiliation in the entire Okarche Region, still predominantly on the Cheyenne-Arapaho tracts, with a total
population of 850 including the few German families
living in town (Figure 11). The age-sex structure of
this population appears more balanced and has the beginnings of a fully pyramidal form. The sex ratio of the
1900 Germans was 116:100, most of the imbalance occur-
ring in the 45-and-older cohorts. The people of German
background comprised 31.6% of the total population of
the region (2,691 people are listed in the 1900 census
for the four-township area, including the town).

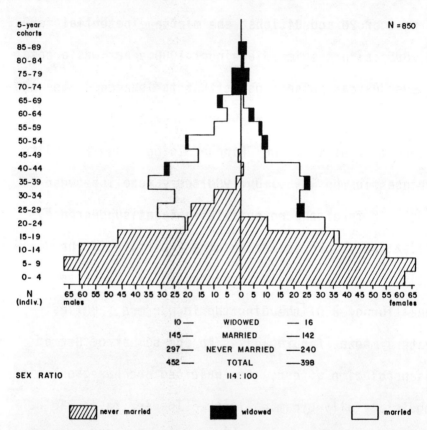

Figure 11. Age-sex profile of the "German" population of Okarche, including all members of immigrant and
German-American households in Okarche center and the
four surrounding townships in 1900 (compiled from the
manuscript schedules of the 1900 census).

It is clear from the size of the 15-19 cohort, as well as from the large number of unmarried males between the ages of 20 and 34, that the marriage potential for the Germans in the immediate post-1900 years was great. The age-sex data also suggest that the standard ages at marriage for German women were between 20 and 24. This is true also of the population at large. Age at marriage for men was slightly older, usually between 25 and 29. Some of the potential marriages suggested by age-sex data took place soon after the turn of the century, beginning what was to become the major generational turnover of the First World War era. But even greater impetus for increases in the number of German households came with new immigration to the region immediately prior to the First World War, involving families originally located in central Midwest states.

One indication of the relative proportions of German and non-German population over a longer span of time can be obtained by viewing cemetery populations. Since the

basic age characteristics of the settlement population
of Okarche were similar throughout all groups, a comparison of deaths in ten-year intervals shows differences
in population size, even in light of turnover processes.
The Germans, moreover, maintained cemeteries for members
of their two dominant church congregations. Of these,
the Catholic cemetery includes a large number of Irish
and other non-German individuals; therefore, the
Lutheran Cemetery provides a slightly better gross
comparison with the Okarche Cemetery, the overwhelmingly
non-German burial area. The number of burials for the
Lutheran cemetery compared with Okarche cemetery are as
follows:

	Lutheran	Okarche
1893-1902	8	31
1903-1912	14	33
1913-1922	25	27
1923-1932	19	17
1933-1942	26	6

| 1943-1952 | 36 | 14 |
| 1953-1962 | 24 | 10 |

Both cemetery populations show fluctuations resulting from the initial asymmetrical conditions of the settlement population. However, in spite of the fact that between 1923 and 1932 the majority of the eldest original settlers had already died (those who had been over 49 in 1892), the Lutheran cemetery reflects a population of equivalent size to the non-German cemetery. The Lutherans from that time through the present represent only one-third to one-half of the total population of Okarche of German background. Thus, after 1932 Okarche may be said to have begun tending toward its present situation. At that time the overall population of the region was dominated by people of German background, and the German component of the town was beginning to increase dramatically.

The turnover period of Okarche history represents more than the simple adjustment of families on the land

during the first four to five years of settlement. That
period, especially for the Cheyenne-Arapaho run, was
certainly of importance, but continued in and out migrations of households resulted in German dominance over
the region. After 1900, the transfer of only a few
quarter-sections per year subtly transformed the character of the town and countryside. Of course, other
events and conditions contributed to this process, and
these are the subject of other parts of this work. But
the demographic changes in early Okarche present the
clearest picture of the scale and direction of overall
processes operative in the community. At worst, they
represent an ample basis for social and economic
analysis. It is helpful, then, to add a few other
threads of demographic information pertinent to later
Okarche and summarize processes which helped to shape
the community through the late 1930's.

SUMMARY OF DEMOGRAPHIC TRENDS

It is clear that the two settlement areas which ultimately formed parts of the Okarche region underwent similar demographic processes. Even though the Oklahoma and Cheyenne-Arapaho run areas manifest different patterns of age-sex distribution, their composite characteristics become relatively well-balanced by or shortly after 1900. It is therefore possible to list the basic features of the processes involved in the early settlement sequence, and thereby project some of the potentials for stable population characteristics that follow the settlement period, given alternative economic conditions. A basic scenario for the demographic changes in Okarche includes:

(1) The establishment of a young, predominantly male population, including many single adults and young married couples, on initial claims of unimproved land.

(2) Selection against single claimants and couples in the rural sector, in favor of larger households, resulting in rapid turnover and the introduction of new young population.

(3) Relatively early inclusion of old persons as attached members of households, resulting in a rapid, short-term overall increase in extended family households.

(4) An initially high fertility rate which persists for only a few years, reflecting the young of the initial adult settlers.

(5) A gradual balancing of the sex ratios of the overall population throughout the turnover period, with more stable ratios being manifested as continuity on the land is established.

(6) The establishment of fertility, in spite of the reduction of births to the maturing households, as the prime impetus for population growth after the initial high-turnover period.

(7) Net increases in the number of people and proportions of households of German background, mainly in the rural sector, through the 1930's.

(8) A change in the nature of extended family households reflecting reductions (through mortality) in the number of households including elderly parents of claimants, and increases (through marriage of children) in three-generation households of elderly claimants.

(9) A secondary formation of family/farm networks including splinter households stemming from initial settler families, also commencing as the elder cohorts of settler children reach marriage age.

(10) A second onset of high fertility as greater numbers of marriages occur, and the stabilization of birthrates commencing with these marriages.

(11) Increased pressure of land resulting in household extension and out-migration, alleviated to some extent by the onset of deaths or retirement of the initial parental cohorts, beginning approximately 20

years after settlement and continuing through the late
1930's.

(12) Ultimate displacement of the more youthful
town population as elderly farmers retire to town, and
economic depression takes hold.

Some of the general demographic trends noted by
Lefferts (1977) for frontier situations are reflected in
these specific Okarche trends. The overall processes
seem to be somewhat "compressed" in time relative to
other frontiers, if indeed we are correct in calling
Oklahoma settlement a frontier situation. It is
evident, however, that the scale of Oklahoma settlement
was quite different than that of the east coast, for
example, or the old Northwest, northern plains areas,
and Texas settlement of later times. This difference in
both population size, general competition for land,
logistics, and temporal placement tended to speed
processes of demographic adjustment which took longer
periods of time in other American settlement areas.

Given the rather rapid achievement of stability on the Oklahoma frontier, the transition of land from parents to children is among the most important demographic factors affecting social and economic life in Okarche. This is perhaps more true than in other frontier situations we might view because the "pioneer period" did not last through the lifespans of the initial settlers. Thus, as a final note on demographic trends in Okarche it is necessary to view the timing of the generational transitions more closely, again relying primarily on cemetery data. Figure 12 shows deaths in the Lutheran cemetery population from 1892 through 1962, arranged in ten-year cohorts reflecting birthdates. The beginning of the first generational transition is seen between 1913 and 1922, with eight deaths of individuals who had been 20 to 49 years of age in 1892. In the subsequent decade the youngest of these cohorts (20-29 in 1892) entered its sixties, so deaths and retirements of the whole group opened numerous farms to the next

Age in 1892	over-49	40-49	30-39	20-29	10-19	0-9								total
Birthdate Span	1842 & earlier	1843–1852	1853–1862	1863–1872	1873–1882	1883–1892	1893–1902	1903–1912	1913–1922	1923–1932	1933–1942	1943–1952	1953–1962	
1893–1902	1	3				1	3							8
1903–1912	5	2	1	4	1	1								14
1913–1922	5		4	4	1	1	1	1	8					25
1923–1932	3	1	3	3			1	3	3	2				19
1933–1942		3	8			5	3	3		1	3			26
1943–1952		1	3	9	10	5	4	2				2		36
1953–1962			1	2	4	6	2	4		1			4	24
totals	14	10	20	22	16	19	14	13	11	4	3	2	4	152

year of death

Figure 12. Mortality of the Lutheran Cemetery Population from 1892 through 1962 arranged in ten-year cohorts and ten-year intervals (compiled from information reported by Stallings, Stallings, and Conover 1964).

generation. A similar transition began during the period of the Second World War, involving deaths of people who had been born between 1902 and 1873.

These generational cycles correspond closely to technological transformations in agriculture (see Chapter IV). They also begin during the two war periods. Thus, the initial settler, first-generation, and second-generation Okarche farmers fall temporally into distinctive familial and techno-economic patterns. They also manifest distinctive outlooks on a social and cultural front. For example, transformations of language use--and therefore, one of the prime mechanisms of social bounding operative in early Okarche--match the generational turnover closely. The subsequent sections of this work, then, make use of the isomorphy of demographic-technological-economic-social sequencing in the presentation of material. Indeed, it is difficult to resist such treatment of material which offers itself to a contrapuntal style. However, it should also be

noted that the apparent synchronization of the two wars
suggested in the treatment is fortuitous. It was determined largely by the age of the settlement population
and time of settlement. For this reason, we will
concentrate on the changing population as a primary
causal factor in viewing the transformations of agriculture, social bounding, and cultural identity in Okarche,
rather than centering on the widely believed "impacts"
of the wars on Germans in the United States. This
approach will show that the importance of the anti-
German sentiment of the war years to life in Okarche was
minimal, and perhaps over-rated in other parts of the
United States as well. At the least, it is to be
expected that multiple factors of local social and
economic organization, from the level of households to
the community as a whole, would provide the only milieu
in which generalized pressures of anti-German feeling
could induce change.

CHAPTER IV

LONG-TERM ECONOMIC DEVELOPMENT IN OKARCHE

ECONOMIC STRUCTURES

The economic structure of early small communities in Oklahoma was quite different from that of today. In centers such as Okarche, for example, a much broader range of occupations was pursued, and hence a broader range of services was available to both town and rural people. Non-agricultural services and agricultural supplies were locally available to a ready rural population, and the town served as a major market place for the products of the land. The main exceptions to this service and commodity pattern were wheat and cotton, key products directed to national markets by rail. Thus, there was a "productive" division between town and countryside that does not exist today. The long-term transition in the town has reduced services offered and

brought a loss of local hold on consumers. The technology of communication has changed with the development
of the state, and many interactional and economic functions of the old community have been taken over by other
places in the region.

In the rural theater there has been a transition
from small-scale farming to specialized wheat production. This development is closely intertwined with the
changes of the town proper and is reflected strongly in
the demographic history of the community. In particular, the town is now made up of families of rural
association, both retired and young farmers. Indeed,
the rural limits of the Okarche service area have been
somewhat redefined by this change in the town's population, so Okarche embraces a much small territory and
much more well-defined social units.

One might expect that the social economic growth of
any community would involve a crystallization process--a
definitive development following specific rules of

"bonding" in its internal sphere, but also individually shaped by the general constraints of large contexts. This is precisely the case in Okarche; for what began as a loosely organized and varied collection of families, occupations, backgrounds, and approaches to economic success became a well-organized and highly patterned set of social units specifically tied to each other and the central place. And as this process continued, the "economic" functions of the community became highly specialized--"fit," so to speak, to the other social institutions of the whole and the larger economic field of central Oklahoma. In order to understand such a process, however, it is insufficient to describe it as a series of events. The events, as Braudel (1972) and Wallerstein (1974) have both recently suggested, must be given meaning in terms of the structures which "impede" and "control" them. Thus, a history must have its time-less sense, and speak to the _form_ which is embedded in the action of its _content_. If we are concerned with

structures or cycles in history, then we are also
concerned with the master framings of time which carry
meaning to us for the events of daily life.

Thus, we may focus upon particular patterns of
activity in an abstract sense. In Okarche the basic
agricultural system may be represented as a succession
of three such abstract forms--the "yearly round" of the
horse farm, the small-tractor farm, and the large-
tractor farm. Each of these forms held sway for some
major period during the past 85 years; each has its own
logic and implications. These may in turn be analysed
in terms of their relations to broader patterns of
family growth, demographic change on the community
level, cycles of war and peace, and patterns of prosper-
ity and depression. And so we may also see the yearly
agricultural round as a series of time-bound events, the
peculiar twists of each new waxing and waning of
activity reflecting the place of repetition in the
larger flow of time, and the circumstances locked with

it in a particular present. It is in this way that we arrive at larger patterns of "growth" and "decline" which we call processes and which represent the conjuncture of many scales of systemic operation.

YEARLY FARMING CYCLES

The yearly cycle of the horse farm is depicted in Figure 13. The general division of activities shown in the schematic representation is between (1) seasonal activities, and (2) male and female activities. The "seasons" are defined by their associated work, and so do not represent arbitrary calendrical units. Thus, the "winter" activities begin in late October or early November and last through perhaps late February, "spring" activities continue through early June, and "summer" encompasses the whole harvest period through late August. The short "fall transition" identifies the

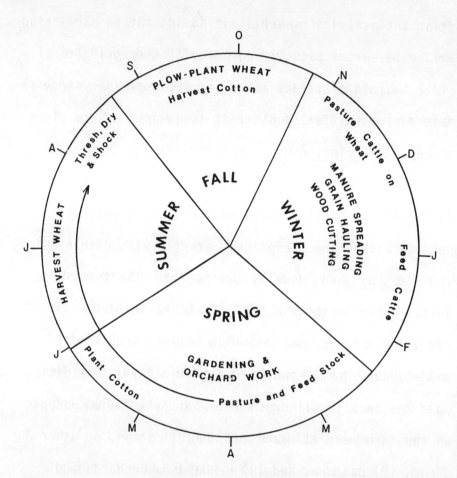

Figure 13. The yearly cycle of work activities on
the horse farm (primary activities in all-caps; important
secondary activities shown in upper-lower case lettering).

important period of wheat planting and cotton harvesting and represents a natural beginning of the agricultural cycle. Since decisions about the whole coming year were made during the fall months, it is an appropriate place to begin description.

It is important to understand the scale of the horse farm. The settlers of the land runs and homestead period, with a few exceptions, started with either 80 or 160 acres of land, usually the latter. The farms were quite varied in their position relative to water resources, and to some degree in their initial soil conditions. Most, however, were run without irrigation on a reasonably well-drained soil base. The components of the farm were (1) land for wheat, cotton, or other crops, (2) pasture, and (3) orchards. Orchards and pasture represent a set commitment of space, so that an average farm in 1900 included only about 50 acres of cultivated area for wheat, oats, cotton, and vegetables (Abstract of the Twelfth Census, 1900: 217). The

optimal condition of land commitment was to have about
one-half of the farm cultivated, with the remainder in
use as pasture and orchard (this assessment by an
elderly Okarchean is in substantial agreement with
practice reflected in Twelfth Census of the United
States: Statistical Atlas: Pls. 146-159). Thus, during
the adjustment phase of settlement, a farmer attempted
to build toward a position in which about 80 acres out
of a quarter section could be committed to grain and
other crops.

The horse-drawn plow, in its standard form involving
a four-horse team, was used to prepare fields. One man
and a team could plow about 7 acres per day on the
average, so a single plowing of cultivated land on most
farms took 10 to 15 man-days. Preparation for planting
took place as soon as possible after harvest. The
shifting fronts between northern and southern air masses
provided a reasonably certain period of rain during
September and October, allowing a wheat crop set in

early Fall a good start before the winter. Cotton was not a major crop in Oklahoma until some time after settlement, although some cotton production was begun during the settlement period in Okarche (see Fite 1966: 213; Haystead and Fite 1955: 204-5). Those farms with cotton crops were also involved in harvest in late September and October.

The rule for winter wheat was "sow September, wheat November," and the early growing crop was put to use as pasture during the busy start of the winter (see Okarche Times, Jan. 1895). The winter months were occupied with field maintenance, marketing, and provisioning activities. Manure from cows, horses, and chickens was spread, and hay was stored for the later, colder months. Men also cut poles from an area several miles west of town known as the "blackjacks." These poles were hauled into town where they were reduced for use as fuel. Grain which had been stored at farms after harvest was brought into town to be shipped out to markets by rail.

Women did a great deal of beef canning during the
winter, as well as other farm chores. Dairy cattle were
important in early Okarche and remained prominent until
well into the 1930's. Farms provided cream for
processing in the local creamery during the period from
1906 through the early 1920's, and later the cream was
transported to Enid for processing (Oklahoma Volksblatt,
22 June 1906). Of course, all members of the family
were involved in the care of animals and milking, but
women and children did much of this work when men were
involved in other farming tasks. Most of the clothes of
farmers were made by the women of the household--indeed,
women were probably the busiest contributors to the
farming routine.

During the spring, gardens were planted and much
attention was given to orchard crops. Almost all farms
established orchards which were maintained until the
major drought of the Dust Bowl days. In addition, a few
vineyards were established where soil and water

conditions permitted. Before the Dust Bowl period,

water conditions in central Oklahoma were much more

conducive to these activities. Vegetables and fruit,

including peaches, apples, and pears, contributed to the

local market in the center and home consumption. There

was a concomitant activity of canning and setting

preserves associated with these crops. Animals were

returned to pasture during the spring. Cows were some-

times pastured in common fields which were to be pre-

pared for new crops. They were taken to these fields in

the morning and returned home in the evening by school

children. A boy might make a dollar a month per cow for

performing this service. At the close of spring, cotton

was planted. Again, the size of the cotton crop during

the early years was small, in part because of other

commitments to the land, and in part because of the

continuous cultivation requirements of the crop. The

deleterious effects of cotton on the soil were out-

weighed somewhat by the potential insurance cotton

provided against wheat failure (see Margolis 1977: 617).
In addition, if the wheat crop did not do well in the
spring, farmers sometimes recommitted land to corn.
Corn could be planted in time to take advantage of late
April and early May rains, or even later planting
sometimes provided relief against a major wheat loss.

In June the mature winter-wheat crop was ready to
harvest, and so men were totally involved in the fields.
Women and children took over almost all of the other
farming chores during the harvest period, and, in addition, women cooked for the large harvesting crews. The
harvest routine on the horse-farm included four major
activities. First, binders cut the wheat and left long
bundles in rows in the fields. This was accomplished in
June and early July. Then the bundles were stacked of
"shocked" for drying. This was an activity involving
large crews, and sometimes the population of Okarche
would be doubled through the addition of itinerant
workers during the two-day shocking operation. The

wheat would dry in about one week to ten days, and was then ready for threshing. Threshers were set up in the middle of fields and worked from farm to farm in a circuit. The wheat was loaded onto wagons which carried about 50 bushel loads and transported to barns or directly to town. And so with the harvest, the yearly cycle was complete and farmers began preparations for new planting.

Such a farm produced a balance of vegetable crops and animals suitable for direct consumption or small cash gains, and cash crops of wheat and cotton in good years that provided excellent potentials for profit. Unfortunately, wheat prices remained deflated except during the years of World War I, and the necessary commitment of space to oats and pasture reduced the size of the cash commodities. The diversified farm with 50 to 80 acres in wheat, oats, cotton, and corn, a few milk cows, 80 to 100 chickens, four or dive draft horses or mules, a vegetable garden, an orchard, and a reserve of

pasture land represented, nonetheless, an efficient
operation given labor conditions and commodity prices of
the period. There was flexibility to allow for changing
weather conditions, and reasonable self sufficiency in
the area of energy resources for fuel and animal maintenance.

The winter-wheat specialization of modern times is
an outgrowth of what was earlier an "emphasis" derived
from the experience of farmers in the prairie lands of
Nebraska and Kansas in the 1870's (see Fite 1966:
50-52). Okarche was in an excellent position for wheat
production since it was located on the Rock Island
Railway line. In spite of deflated prices and drought
conditions in 1894 and 1895, the Okarche Times (June 9,
1893) printed pieces encouraging farmers to plant as
much wheat as possible. In actuality, most of the
farmers had a much firmer perception of what was really
going on in the ground, and it is doubtful that these
editorials had much impact on farming practice. More

important were the releases of information about crop
and husbandry research from Oklahoma State Agricultural
Testing Stations, which occurred in all newspapers of
the region during the settlement period. In the
German-language newspaper printed in El Reno there were
similar articles on Obst un Weinbau (Oklahoma Volksblatt, 22 June 1906). A major contributor to these
resided in Okarche and most of the people of German
background subscribed to the paper (see also Willibrand
1951: 290). Such information provided keys to better
management of diversified farms, and thus promoted cropping and husbandry strategies that offered better
opportunities for long-term success.

During the 1920's horses began to be replaced by
small tractors, and a number of changes in the agricultural cycle took place. The basic pattern of the
farming cycle remained almost intact, but the reduction
of the horse population released land which had formerly
been committed to oats, other feed crops, and even

pasture, for use as wheat and cotton fields. It is
during this period that cotton became a major crop in
the Okarche area as well as in other parts of central
Oklahoma (Haystead and Fite 1955, 204-5). Small
tractors (Figure 14) were used in the cultivation of
cotton through the 1930's (Haystead and Fite 1955: 205;
Table 72, 188). Although they were only slightly more
efficient than a horse-team in terms of daily work output, the small tractors afforded relative luxury for the
farmer. Early tractors could work about ten acres per
day and reduced maintenance costs slightly. As time
went on, of course, larger tractors were produced and a
real mechanical commitment was established. But as long
as the tractors were small, they could work under much
the same conditions as horses and produced a similar
scale of results.

Along with the small-tractor farm came the beginning
of a major husbandry shift in the Okarche region. By
the 1930's more land was being committed to crops and

Figure 14. Small tractors cultivating cotton in the Okarche region sometime during the early 1920's (photograph courtesy of Frank Heinen).

there was stress on land used for the maintenance of cattle. It is during the 1930's and 1940's then, that beef cattle began to replace dairy cattle in the area (see Indian Pioneer Papers for statements on Okarche and early beef cattle). Beef cattle could be raised and sold, rather than requiring maintenance throughout the year. One could keep them or not, according to other farming circumstances, and thus control land use during different parts of the yearly cycle. This shift was not fully felt until after World War II, but it represents a second chink in the generalized position of the early community.

We may see the small tractor period, then, as one in which there were: (1) greater commitments to specialization in cash crops--either cotton or wheat, (2) reduction in the reliance upon dairy production as a cash-producing activity, (3) more complete cropping of land, and (4) greater reliance upon energy resources external to the farmer's direct control, specifically upon the growing petro-chemical industry. This last trend involved both fuel and fertilizer, and represents perhaps the most significant departure from the practice of former years.

The small-tractor farm was heavily impacted by the depression and drought of the 1930's. Although the effects of the Dust Bowl were not as severe in central Oklahoma as they were farther to the west, the combination of circumstances of the period brought a quick end to the heavy cotton emphasis in central oklahoma (Haystead and Fite 1955: 204-7). There was not a change in the trends toward specialization of cropping, or toward mechanization. During World War II and after, there was a complete return to wheat on central Oklahoma farms; the land was denuded of orchards and partically depleted by the cotton boom, but chemical fertilization and a new scale of operation contributed to the success of the endeavor.

The immediate post-war period brought major technological shifts in both the farming cycle and the general
communication system of the region. Whereas a trip to
Oklahoma City in the 1920's took two days by wagon,
general use of trucks and improved roads greatly
increased the farmer's potential to deal directly with
markets in the region--today, the trip takes only 30 to
40 minutes. On the farm, large tractors capable of
working several hundred acres per day are the rule, and
the harvest is accomplished by locally owned and
contracted combines. These giants, representing investments of about $45,000.00 each, cut and thresh the wheat
in the Okarche district in a scant 10 days. Working day
and night, the town turns its total attention to the
crop, just as in years past, but with a new intensity
and flourish.

The contemporary wheat farm is striking in that it
is large and may be adequately worked by an individual
with minimal help except during harvest. A "break-even"

point for a wheat farm today requires probably two quarter-sections, but most farms involve three or four quarters and many are much larger than that. Some farmers have other occupations which supplement earnings from grain production, or against which wheat profits are supplemental. But the importance of timing in the yearly cycle is still great. Too much rain during the harvest, for example, can result in serious crop losses or severe labor shortages. Crop loss means the loss of thousands of dollars. Delay because of rain or other factors during the harvest of a particular area puts strain on the overall harvest schedule since contracted combines move north from southern Oklahoma and the Texas panhandle through Kansas and into Nebraska. The sheer bulk of combines prohibits harvesting in very wet conditions, and the wheat itself must be dry in order to insure maximum yield. So weather conditions, more than ever before, are critical to farming success.

Considering the investment required to maintain a farm and produce a crop, it is not surprising to find a busy yearly schedule. The investment includes equipment, fuel, fertilizer, insecticides, contracted costs of other commodities and services which sustain the farmer but are no longer produced by the household. But the schedule does not involve many small-scale activities each of which contributes in a different way to sustenance and cost production. Rather, longer periods of time are taken up in the performance of tasks that all contribute to the wheat crop.

The large-tractor farm, then, is a specialized concern in both ecological and economic terms. The wheat fields replicate the kind of "grassland" conditions which typified the area of Okarche before settlement. Beef cattle, when they are kept, represent larger and more concentrated populations than the individual dairy interests of the generalized early form of farm organization. Wheat farmers are also inextricably tied to the major commodity structures of the nation and world. World demand for grain, coupled with the success of farming technology in the United States, allows the Oklahoma area to produce and favorably market wheat on an amazing scale. Cattle management is fit to the early phase of beef production and articulated with a large feed lot east of town and the stock yards in Oklahoma City. And finally, in recent years work has begun to tap natural gas resources running between Oklahoma City and points to the northwest through the Okarche region, so some farmers are actually producing three of the key commodities in the national and world resource system.

The agricultural development of Okarche has involved a series of economic boundary expansions. It began on a subsistence level and in a trade medium where barter and credit were more important than marketing, and progressed through local, regional, national, and international market postures which influenced the application of technology and constrained family growth. With each new generation in the farming population it became increasingly difficult to acquire land sufficient to employ all of the sons of a particular family, increasingly expensive to procure equipment, and easier to obtain training and employment elsewhere. Thus, while many of the children of the pioneer generation in Okarche remained in the community as farmers, beginning their farms during the period between the two world wars, a much smaller proportion of their children remained. The pressures which produced this situation were augmented by the development of the center itself. We must view that development in order to complete the picture of economic change which has shaped the modern community.

COMMERCIAL DEVELOPMENT IN OKARCHE CENTER

The first townsite lots in Okarche were obtained in El Reno on a cash basis, and very quickly businesses were established to provide goods and services necessary to survival in the region. A 30 ft. by 150 ft. lot in the center sold for $75.00 in 1889, considerable investment for most of the settler population. However, a small nucleus of merchants, craftsman, and professionals established themselves on the line separating Kingfisher and Canadian Counties, immediately adjacent to the rail stop of the Rock Island line. Most of the early shops and dealers were in Canadian County, as were the grain elevator, two of the early churches, two schools, and eventually, the post office. At first, mail was received by way of a common box located east of town. Newspaper advertisement of the early 1890's include local and regional establishments, particularly business ads from El Reno and Kingfisher. However, a list of

businesses in Okarche in 1894 depicts the breadth of
occupations of the early center. (Table 5).

The most important early businesses in Okarche were
the bank, insurance company, the lumber companies, and
the general stores. The bank was one of the few establishments founded by a person of German heritage, and is
now the oldest continuously operated enterprise of the
community. Also associated with the German population
was the insurance company (Deutschen Farmers Gegenseiti-
gen Feuer Versicherungs-Verein von Okarche) which also
continues operation today under another name (see
Willibrand 1951: 290). In 1894 there were two lumber
companies and five general stores, the former supplying
construction materials and the latter many of the commodity needs of the rural population. It was sometimes
several years before farmers could make large improve-
ments on their land. But the trade in building
materials thrived throughout the settlement period. In
fact, most of the businesses of the first ten years

bank and insurance office	1
barber	1
butcher shops	2
candy store	1
cobbler	1
dentist	1
drugstore	1
furniture and agricultural implements store	1
grist mill	1
general stores	5
grocery store	1
grain elevator	1
hardware stores	2
harness company	1
harness shop	1
hotels	3
ice house	1
livery	1
lumber yards	2
lunch shop (attached to butcher shop)	1
lunch shop	1
millinery shop	1
paint shop	1
printer	1
saloon	3
school	1
tin shop	1
wagon shop	1

Table 5. Establishments depicted on the Sanborn-Perris Map of Okarche, 1894.

appear to have enjoyed more success than new businesses
do today. Of individuals working in the town and listed
in the 1900 census, several undoubtedly go back to the
first year or two of settlement. The occupations listed
in the census (Table 6) included some not depicted in
the Sanborn-Perris map of 1894--cement workers, editors,
doctors, day laborers, machinists, photographers, a
cheese maker, and a jeweler. In addition, a full range
of jobs associated with such establishments as the
hotels, livery, lumber yards, and agricultural occupations also represent stable population dating to the
earliest settlement.

There were, nevertheless, many failures and changes
of ownership. The newspaper, for example, changed hands
several times in the first 10 years (Willibrand 1951).
It served the English-speaking community, but was a poor
competitor for the German-speaking subscribers of the
area. We have already noted that Germans more often
took the Oklahoma Volksblatt, printed in El Reno, or

Occupation		Occupation	
banker	1	hotel keeper	2
barber	2	jeweler	1
blacksmith	3	livery	1
book keeper	1	lumber dealer	3
brick mason	1	machinist	2
butcher	1	mason	2
carpenter	9	merchant	5
cement workers	9	miller	2
cheese maker	1	minister	7
clerk	2	night watchman	1
collector--real estate	1	photographer	2
cook	1	plasterer	2
day laborer	10	porter	2
doctor	2	RR laborer	8
druggist	2	Restauranteer	1
drygoods merchant	1	salesman	1
drygoods clerk	1	saloon keeper	1
editor	2	stone mason	2
engineer (various)	4	tailor	1
grain dealer	2	teacher	5
grocery clerk	3	teamster	6
grocery merchant	2	telephone man	1
hardware	1	tiner	2
harness dealer	1		
harness maker	1		

Table 6. Occupations listed in the 1900 census in Okarche center and immediately surrounding non-agricultural concerns males; compiled from the manuscript schedules of the 1900 census).

other German language newspapers. Later, as English came into general use in the community, the local paper became a more community-wide vehicle for information transmission. Thus, Okarche never supported a local German-language paper. The fact that the early papers continued to operate indicates the size of the early non-German population, especially in the center. Individuals also sometimes made several attempts at starting a business, or were involved in more than one enterprise. There is one interesting series of notes in the Okarche Times, running over a several month period, which places an individual first on a farm southwest of town, later as a partner in a saloon, and finally as an outmigrant to accept a railroad job in Kansas City.

During the early 1900's a creamery was established in Okarche. A note in the El Reno newspaper tells us that the Gesellschaft zur Fabrikation von Butter und Kase collected a capital base of $25,000.00, and began production in 1906 (Oklahoma Volksblatt, 22 June 1906).

The creamery continued in operation until the early
1920's. In a monthly report for 1914 (Okarche Times,
January 1914), a list of contributors and dollar values
for their monthly production is given. This list was
used to encourage support of the operation. The
individual cash payments listed for the month ranged
from $68.15 to just over $20.00 from four cows' production over the month. The overall volume of the creamery
was great. It processed 19,415 pounds of cream in
January 1914, produced 6,920 pounds of butter. The
cream payments for the month totaled almost $1,500.00.
This represents a production of from 1,500 to 1,800
pounds of butter per week. An indication of the importance of the German-speaking community in Okarche is
given in this record. Only one of the top twenty cream
producers among the farmers was not of German background, and most of those listed represent families
still in the community today. This is one of the few
direct economic indications of the important post-1900
influx of German families.

The fortunes of businessmen of the center were
dependent upon the success of the agricultural community, and the period of the 1930's affected the center
dramatically. After the depression there were no longer
hotels, the creamery had closed, and many of the non-
German small merchants had left the community. There
was a long-term resident doctor in Okarche who came in
the early 1930's when individuals from the community
finally got an Oklahoma City physician to take up residence in the area. A rather typical small-town pattern
of retirement into the center began during the 1920's
and continued through this period to today.

A list of contemporary establishments in the town of
Okarche (Table 7) suggests the two major specializations
of the center--medical services and agricultural support
facilities. Many of the businessmen in town also farm.
Through the efforts of the banker and the doctor, the
Okarche community hospital was established after the
War. This enterprise enjoyed wide community support

Antique Store	1
Automobile Dealers	2
Agricultural Supply Companies	3
Bank	1
Bar	1
Beauty Salon	1
Butane Dealer	1
Clinic	1
Club	1
Cooperative	1
Drive-in Restaurant	1
Flower Shop	1
Funeral Home	1
Grain Company	1
Grass Equipment Company	1
Grocery Stores	2
Hospital	1
Insurance Office	1
Lumber Company	1
Motel	1
Package Store	1
Pharmacy	1
Service Stations	2
Small Industrial Corporation	1
Schools	3

        Catholic (1-8)
        Lutheran (1-8)
        Public   (K-12)
Other Listings
        Volunteer Fire Department
        Town Office
        Post Office

Table 7. Contemporary businesss and public establishments in Okarche (compiled from information gained in a survey of places made by the investigator and from listings in the Okarche telephone directory).

from the beginning and is administered by Sisters of the Felician Order. The hospital and clinic were a wider area than other establishments in Okarche today, although the automobile dealers enjoy overhead advantages over the major dealers of Oklahoma City, and therefore, do some regional business. All of the other businesses are much more local in their orientation, serving the people of the town and the immediately adjacent countryside. The only businesses with potential for transient earnings are the motel and two eating establishments.

Almost immediately after settlement, schools were established by the Lutherans and the Catholics, in addition to the public school. The Catholic school took students from grades one through twelve, as did the public school. The Lutheran school operated with grades one through eight, and for a time had kindergarten classes. The kindergarten was discontinued after one was established in the public school. The two church

schools now operate classes through the eighth grade,
and the public schools takes all of the high-school
students. The operation of three separate school
systems in a town with such a small population base is
unusual. Indeed, it is rather unique even among German
communities of Oklahoma. This in part accounts for the
large number of teachers in the 1900 census population
(see Table 6). In addition, because of the expense
involved, it suggests the degree of economic solvency of
Okarche throughout its history. It also suggests a
fundamental aspect of the development of the community.
All of the enterprises established in common by the
German-speakers in Okarche, including the bank and with
the exception of the creamery, have continued operation
uninterrupted from their founding through the present.
Thus, the German-population shared in a wide variety of
resources through the two dominant church groups of the
early era. There remained a strong social boundary
between the Catholics and Lutherans in Okarche, however,

and so the resource groups they represent are somewhat
independent. Many friendships, nonetheless, have
bridged the two groups, and common action of the community as a whole is reflected in the hospital and clinic
establishments. But in business there has at times been
restraint between the member of different congregations.

Probably the major key to the success of the German
population was that it goals, primarily centered on
agriculture, fit well with the larger system of economic
growth in Oklahoma. It was highly unlikely at the time
of Okarche's founding, given the prior establishment of
towns such as El Reno, Kingfisher, and especially
Oklahoma City, that it would become a major commercial
center. It was simply too close to the two county seats
to compete on a wide commercial front, and its location
on a county line worked against its growth. Given a
roughly equal start on the land, then, we would expect
organized groups to compete well against individuals and
small groups of kin. Therefore, German identity aided

farmers in the settlement population to the extent they were associated with that identity in the church congregations. It provided access to support during lean times, labor during critical periods of farming activity, and "familial" identity through the church. And as transportation improved in the region, the services of the town were diminished.

SUMMARY OF ECONOMIC TRENDS

The town of Okarche began as a general-service support center oriented to a local town-based and rural marketing region. The support area was restricted on the north and south by Kingfisher and El Reno. Most of the large capital investments and major support businesses--including the bank, insurance company, creamery, schools, and one of the merchants--were controlled or instigated by people of German background.

The newspaper, a cement works southwest of town, the
hotels, and several small businesses, represented the
non-German population. By the 1920's German farmers
were established in the rural area and were beginning to
retire to town, while the general-service posture of the
commercial sector in town was transformed to a much more
limited set of services. Major enterprises after the
1920's such as the Community Hospital, clinic, auto
dealerships, and the coop, reflect either all-German or
German family actions. The modern center, then, is a
special-service center serving essentially agricultural
and health-care needs of the people. There is, however,
regional support of the hospital and auto dealerships.

In the agricultural sector there had been stead
implementation of capital intensive farming techniques
since the 1920's. This has been reflected also in
specialization of agricultural interests. Therefore,
the patterns of familial continuity have not been manifested in the same manner during the successive

generational turnovers. During the first turnover period, corresponding also to the transformation from horse farms to small-tractor farms, most of the children establishing households became farmers. During the next turnover, however, fewer new farms were established and a major trend of outmigration was established. Thus, the regional and town-based age-sex profiles now reflect a larger proportion of older population.

Okarche farmers saw the last years in which the Oklahoma prairie was used as a ground for specialized beef production. Settlement curtailed that activity within a few years, and beef marketing from the region did not commence again until transportation systems were well developed and the farmers had begun to adopt specialized wheat production as their major agricultural strategy. Beef cattle are very important in the region today, and are gaining in significance slightly as difficulties in the wheat market continue. During the interim period from about 1900 until just before World

War II, dairy and dual-purpose cattle were raised on a small scale. It is also during this period that cotton production began to increase in Oklahoma, affect the Okarche area during the 1920's and 30's.

Generational change matches closely the periods of economic reorientation in Okarche. The pressures for modification of town services stem as much from the changing age characteristics of the town population as they do from general economic circumstances of the state and nation. The modifications of farming technology and new crop selection patterns, moreover, result from the receptivity of newly established farmers and from the climate of the commodities markets and the development of new technology. At the same time, however, larger systemic conditions did influence the nature of the generational changes. So it is impossible to say that familial continuity and generational turnover caused the reorientations any more than one could say just the opposite. The decisions that were made by individuals and small groups concerning practical daily and yearly routines carried an ultimate impact for family structure and continuity in the Okarche community. Those decisions, such as the adoption of cotton as a major crop, did not always operate to the benefit of a family or toward familial continuity on the land. In the end, supports within the community through the churches, the bank, and cooperative organizations favored continuity, providing a safety valve working against failures stemming from poor markets and crop failures. And at the very points when young people were not able to enter the local system and make a living, there were opportunities outside the local system that could take up the excess population. All that was necessary was that children take advantage of their options.

CHAPTER V

SOCIAL UNITS IN OKARCHE: FORMATION AND TRANSFORMATION

ETHNIC ASSOCIATION

In the preceding chapters it was shown that a
sizable foreign-born and first generation German population established itself in the Okarche region during the
first ten years after the opening of the Unassigned
Lands. This population was different from the other
settlers in matters of "background" and "heritage."
All, however, shared a common experience of migration
within North America and activity on the farming
frontiers of the United States between the years following the Civil War and the opening of Oklahoma. In addition, the family circumstances and general population
characteristics did not differ between the German and
non-German segments of the community. All of the
settler groups reflect the same demographic processes

during the critical adjustment period of settlement.
Germans and non-Germans left the community, and many
households of both groups remained.

The German families, however, shared a visibility in
the early community of Okarche which was manifested in
three major ways. First, both foreign-born and
American-born persons of North European heritage spoke
German or a closely related language at the time of
settlement. Most were bilingual, to be sure, but the
majority of these people had learned German as their
primary language, and continued to use it in the home
and in dealings with each other in the town. Further,
early records of the bank and insurance company were in
German, and the services of the Lutheran, Catholic, and
Mennonite churches were conducted in German.

Second, most of the German families were associated
with either the Catholic or Lutheran congregations.
Therefore, a religious demarcation along lines of
heritage existed which not only served to render

"Germans" socially identifiable, but which also segregated these people into resource groups. The interaction between the groups has been variable through the
years, but marriage, land dealings, language use, and to
a degree economic cooperation, have been strongly
influenced by religious differences.

Third, the German families were predominantly rural.
Thus, with few exceptions the early history of Okarche
sees the town dwelling population as distinctively
Anglo-American. The exceptions are notable, however,
including the banker and one of the grocery merchants.
The Anglo-American identity in Okarche was not, however,
as cohesive as were the various identities comprising
the "German" population. The major manifestation of
power relationships in the early town was the Commercial
Club, but this organization did not mediate all aspects
of association for its members to the same extent that
the essentially religious enclaves of the German population did.

Other groups were defined primarily on the basis of religious association. The Mennonites founded a church four miles south of Okarche, around which Mennonite homesteads were established by people of Swiss, German, English, and east-European Germanic heritage. These people interacted much less with townspeople than did other groups, and the locations of the congregation on the ground placed the service area of the church on the boundary of the commercial service areas of Okarche and El Reno. There were also (1) a small group of German Evangelicals, (2) an enclave of Blacks to the east of town who founded their own church, and (3) several other small rural congregations of various denominations. In town the largest non-German church was that of the Congregationalists.

Three of the congregations of the area were part of large regional or national organizations--the Catholic church, the Missouri Lutheran Synod, and the Mennonite church. The other churches were not strongly tied to larger organizations, and so were more totally dependent upon contributions from within for support. The St. John's Lutheran congregation of Okarche, however, was financially supported in part during its first eight years by the Kansas Mission Board of the Missouri Synod (Petrowski 1974: 83-4). Similar supports in the way of clergy and building funds were provided for Holy Trinity Catholic church through the Oklahoma Diocese centered in Oklahoma City.

The Blacks and Indians of the immediate Okarche area formed locational enclaves, while the remainder of the population was spatially more dispersed. Even the Mennonites, who established a relatively tight cluster of homesteads near their church location, were spread across the landscape. It was difficult for large groups to satisfy requirements of soil and water in the selection of a homestead, and at the same time worry about the denomination of one's neighbors or proximity to friends and relatives. This is especially true during the later part of the turnover period, during which many kind related household networks were established. Further, when related families filed independent claims, whether co-located or not, the dates of filing given in the Oklahoma Tract Book are different by months. Thus, the conditions of land acquisition in Oklahoma worked against the creation of large spatial enclaves, such as are observed in the religiously-defined or ethnicly-based communities of the East and Midwest during the 17th through 19th centuries, or in Texas during the 19th and 20th centuries (see Jordan 1966; Gilbert 1971, 1972).

The Mennonite cemetery is located adjacent to the church. It includes two grave groups, one on the north of the church property and the second behind the church to the west. All of the individuals buried in the north grave group represent families that homesteaded in the Okarche area, most in Rock Island and Cement townships during the Cheyenne-Arapaho run. None of the

individuals in the other grave group, however, are
listed in either census or tract materials of the
Okarche study area, except the minister who was a
boarder in a household across the road from the church.
The locations of homesteads of the Mennonites in Rock
Island township are depicted in Figure 15, a sequential
representation of Mennonite, Black, Indian, Catholic,
and Lutheran founder-families that remained in the
region throughout the homestead era. Burials in the
Mennonite cemetery have continued since the last
services were held in the church in 1953, largely
through the completion of family plots. The church and
graveyard are now maintained by the national organizations of the Mennonites.

The two black families shown in Figure 15 on the
east edge of the study area are part of a larger enclave
of blacks centered more to the east. Indian allotments
extended west and southwest from the four shown in the
northwest corner of Harrison township, through Park

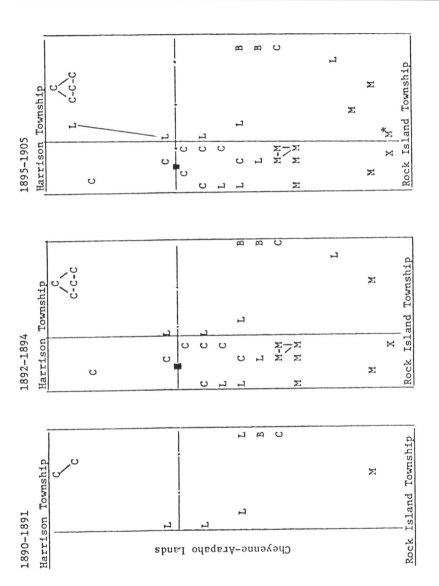

Figure 15. Founder families of German Catholics
and Lutherans, and Mennonites of the North Cemetery group
from 1890 through 1905 in Harrison and Rock Island Townships (I = Indians, B = Blacks, C = Catholics, L =
Lutherans, M = Mennonites, X = Mennonite Church,
* Mennonite minister; Catholics and Lutherans include
families still in Okarche; compiled from Oklahoma Tract
Book).

Township. Between the Mennonites, Blacks, and Indians, especially on the south and west, were Lutheran and Catholic families of German background. There were very few consanguineal family networks during the first ten years in the Oklahoma land run area. The brother of one of the Lutheran founders established an 80-acre farm as a new claimant in 1900. One Catholic family network (brothers and sisters) managed to acquire closely co-located farms and to extend the co-located network after 1892. However, in this case, the extension involved 80-acre tracts rather than 160-acre tracts.

It is apparent that the majority of Germans of both major congregations were part of the Cheynne-Arapaho run, just as was indicated for people of German background in the general demographic discussion (see again Figure 10, Chapter 3). But for the Lutheran congregation, a major growth occurred between 1910 and 1920 with new arrivals from the upper Midwest. This is reflected in marriages of the Lutheran congregation as seen through the burial population. Of 21 women who were born between 1880 and 1900 and who were later buried in the cemetery or had obtained plots with their husbands, only four were related to founder families. Only three of these women were listed in the 1900 census. Moreover, they were all daughters of 1889 settlers, and their families had all been instrumental in the foundation of the church. The other women of this group had all come to Okarche from other localities in the immediate region through marriage or as unmarried members of later migrant families.

The three women just noted represent the three initial Lutheran families depicted in Rock Island township in the 1889 area on Figure 15 b and c. Their marriages tied these families strongly to each other and reflect one of the basic characteristics of the developing frontier. That is, through time there is an increased tendency of families to stay in a frontier area as they develop affinal ties with other families.

The churches formed the basis for a kind of dual
"affinal" tie. Since the number of actual marriages
which occurred within either the Lutheran or Catholic
congregations remained small during the early years of
settlement, the church itself established a symbolic
familial tie within each congregation. The primary
sphere of cooperation for Lutheran and Catholic settlers
was the immediate conjugal family unit, but the strong-
est external sphere of cooperation was the church
congregation. The nexus of resource relationships for
each family incorporated German-speaking people of
similar religious affiliation. The association was
stronger than immediate-neighbor ties, or individual
commercial links into the center. This is especially
true of the Lutherans, but well reflected in the
Catholics of all backgrounds--the Catholic resource
group included several Irish families. The congregations became preferential endogamous groups, since even
before families were actually united through marriages

the corporate nature of the groups was established. The two churches operated their own schools and charitable organizations, as well as maintaining separate cemeteries. Thus, the German community was bipolar, consisting of two well-defined and to some extent competing entities.

These groups were not only bounded from outsiders by denominational difference, but also by language. Lack of knowledge of German immediately excluded a large part of the remaining population of Okarche from some social interactions. German language use in the community, then, became the basis for a level of unity, largely economic, which crossed denominational lines. The cooperative ventures of the insurance company, and later the creamery, were both "German" enterprises. To speak of the "Germans" of Okarche, however, is to recognize an identity viewed mainly from the perspective of the Anglo-American population. From that viewpoint language was an overt manifestation of a generalized cultural

difference, unrecognized as defining a formal
community-wide resource network. It is clear from newspaper materials that Anglo individuals regarded the
"Germans" as different--especially when they were not
incorporated into their circles as were the Irish
Catholics--without realizing the strength of cooperative
bonds and subtleties of differentiation directing social
action in the German-speaking segments of the community.
The success of German farmers became heralded, therefore, as a result of their "hard working" and "moral"
character. These characteristics attributed to Germans
were the source of a great deal of respect on the part
of the Anglo population. There were, nonetheless,
"German" based jokes printed in the early Okarche Times,
and occasional brief notes which indicate a polarity of
German and non-German interests.

In actuality, there was little difference in the
kinds of things Germans and non-Germans did on their
farms, although there were some differences in emphasis.

The most important difference between the Anglo-American population and the German groups was that the Anglo families were not tied to large resource-sharing organizations. Beyond the conjugal family unit, the next most important sphere of cooperation for the Anglo farmers was that of the "farm neighborhood." Cooperation among neighbors in town was less important, however, than the commercial ties of the town leaders in the commercial club, or in independent business links. Even so, the images of the individual, the entrepreneur, or the commercial nucleus that would transform Okarche into a city had less social substance, and less potential given the town's location, than did the simple identities "German," Lutheran, and Catholic.

Another aspect of the economic viability of the German farmers is indicated in the settlement sequence. Many of the German families came to Okarche as second or third claimants and purchased their claims by paying initial homesteaders. Although the Okarche Times generally reflects the activities of the Anglo-American

population, several notes indicate transfers from non-

Germans to German land owners and the amounts paid for

claims. In 1895 between the months of January and April

the following comments were printed in the general news

sections of the paper:

> Peter Schmitz bought John Fox's farm. This
> gives him a half-section (Feb. 22).
>
> August Ingold purchased Daniel Kelley's claim
> located 4 miles south of town for $1800.000
> (Jan. 10).
>
> A. Ingold began building a large house south-
> west of town. (Jan. 24).
>
> Mr. Litwiller purchased 120 acres of land
> adjacent to the town on the Northwest. Mr.
> Ingold, former owner, moved to one of two
> quarters he owns outside town. (April).

These transactions show two instances of non-German

release of farm land. The price of $1,800.00 for a

160-acre claim is similar to other prices noted during

the same period, and in another series of notes we also

see how land became available as a result of family

circumstances:

> Mrs. J. K. Moss died at the home of her
> parents, residing in Missouri. (Jan. 3).

> John Ottis' father has purchased Mr. Moss'
> 120-acre farm adjoining town on the southwest
> for $2000.00. (April 8).

Very few such reported transfers of claim of title show Germans leaving the Okarche area and most involve German buyers either entering the rural sector from the town, or extending their holdings of agricultural land. The Germans who entered the community just before World War I, primarily Lutheran, bought farms with money they had received for their land in the Corn Belt. In some cases they realized a 400% increase of acreage for their dollar investment. Of course, not all of the German settlers had capital resources sufficient to buy claims or established farms, but a substantial number did, creating a long-term trend of transfers into German ownership. Among successful homesteaders the addition of three or four quarter sections within the first twenty to thirty years was common.

Continuance on the land throughout the settlement period and after was a matter of at least meeting subsistence needs. The German resource groups, German-wide economic cooperative ventures, and developing familial ties aided tremendously in riding out stress periods. The more socially "isolated" Anglo families had fewer and more limited tiers of resource support for such periods as well as fewer ties that might make them endure extreme hardships in the interest of staying in Okarche. There were, nonetheless, many families of non-Germans who remained in the Okarche area, some through the present. But these families have come to be less and less "associated" with Okarche. Thus, in addition to German acquisition of the majority of tracts immediately surrounding the town, the German population has become the primary service population of the center.

Changes in the major communication vehicles for the center reflect this trend. The early newspaper was very irregularly read by German families who preferred the

Oklahoma Volksblatt, published in El Reno. By the early
part of this century, however, most of the articles in
the English-language newspaper in Okarche reflect local
German activities. Naturally, the church activities
formed part of the material in the papers between 1905
and 1920, but it is also evident that the economic and
political nucleus of the community was heavily German at
this time. This is in part a result of the location of
the town straddling the boundary of two counties.
Political action of the center engaged people of both
counties, but supports from the county level were
directed from two sources with very poor coordination.
The effective political nexus of the town in this case
mirrored the religious division of Lutheran and Catholic
Germans--these were the groups which could amass
resources for the common good of people with interests
in and around Okarche. Thus, the Germans had political
advantage over the territorially defined governmental
units and people who tried to operate exclusively within
these units.

We see in the early German-speaking population,
then, the basis for economic and political competition
which might account in part for the ultimate success of
German families in Okarche:

(1) The Germans were socially isolated from the
Anglo population, but positively received through the
symbols attached to them by non-Germans. Essentially,
those notions of German religiousness, hard-working
nature, and efficiency fit an Anglo conception of the
ingredients necessary for success as a pioneer (see
Ruth, 1976, for continuity of this view). Furthermore,
the fledgling commercial sector of the town regarded all
agricultural success as a necessary ingredient of their
own viability (Okarche Times, Dec. 8, 1901; see also
Okarche Times, June 9, 1893, for attitudes on the importance of wheat production to the town).

(2) Social isolation of the Germans and the
polarity of Lutherans and Catholics created two effective resource groups which gave German families an

advantage over non-Germans. The exclusivity of these groups was maintained by language and denominational factors; thus, recruitment was generally directed to locations external to the town and region.

(3) Anglo resource networks were more diffuse and fluid and were not mediated by formal organizations which persisted through time. The primary basis of external social resources rested in "neighborly" action or private contracts. Thus, the trend of German recruitment drained social resources in the non-German sphere, except in the case of families attached to the German-Catholic enclave through the church. Recruitment in voluntary associations dominated by Anglo families-- especially the churches, was local, and so also subject to the same pressures. In this situation only the most efficient farmers and businessmen could survive.

(4) The county-line location of Okarche further segmented the Anglo-American population politically, while the German resource groups took on community-wide political functions for their members.

These factors contributed to a situation in which Germans developed greater group commitment, in some cases sacrificing latitude of personal action, but achieved greater flexibility in the area of economic performance on a familial level. On the contrary, the Anglo-American population developed more limited group commitment, or in some cases a strongly idiosyncratic social stance, at a cost of productive flexibility. In this sense, The German organizations were better "adapted" to the Oklahoma frontier situation and the particular climatic and economic events of settlement than were Anglo-Americans.

The long-term result of this situation was the reduction of the number of farms in the region, the creation of larger farms, and the establishment of almost total German dominance of the rural service area of Okarche and its center. Figure 16 shows contemporary farm sites reflected in the telephone directory of Okarche, with families distinguished when possible by

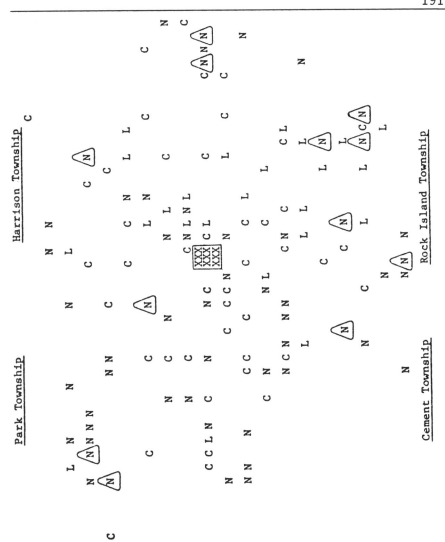

Figure 16. Contemporary farmsties by religious affiliation and background (C = Catholic, L = Lutheran, N = unknown religious affiliation, △ = not of German background, X = town location).

religious affiliation. The area of the rural service region in the figure is a minimum of 130 square miles, and there are 134 families depicted. Several other families could not be plotted, but their addition would probably have extended the land area of the service region. If all of the land in the region were controlled by those farmers living in the rural sector, then the average farm size would be about one square mile. In actuality, there are other farmers who live in town, and land holdings vary considerably. However, contemporary average farm size in the wheat belt of Oklahoma is well over 500 acres (Haystead and Fite 1955: 185-7). The acquisition patterns of the Germans during the early part of the century and the information of Figure 16 both suggest that an average figure of 500 acres in Okarche for contemporary farms is not unreasonable.

Of the 131 farmsteads shown in Figure 16, approximately one-half are included in large family networks.

Contemporary "same-surnamed" farm sites are depicted in
Figure 17. The distribution of networks in the two
settlement areas shows the differential processes
through which German acquisition took place. The
networks are overlapping and dispersed in the Unassigned
lands area, showing long-term acquisitions--especially
of the Lutheran population. On the contrary, the
networks of the Cheyenne-Arapaho lands are more
discrete, indicating co-locations and block acquisition.
Fuller identification of religious background would
probably show a preponderance of Catholic families,
although the apparent preponderance of Catholics in the
western settlement area is most likely a function of
incomplete data.

Firm spatial segregation of Catholics and Lutherans
occurs in the town today. A map of family locations
differentiated by denomination (Figure 18) shows clear
pockets of Lutherans and Catholics on the south side of
town, a mixed area of the west side between the Lutheran

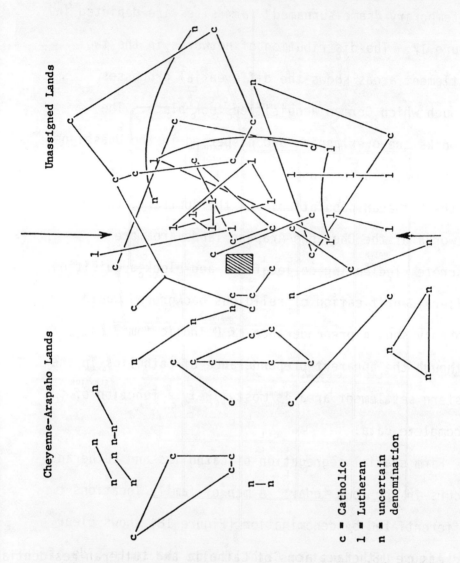

Figure 17. Farmsteads operated by same-surnamed
indviiduals in comtemporary Okarche (compiled from the
address listings of the Okarche telephone listings).

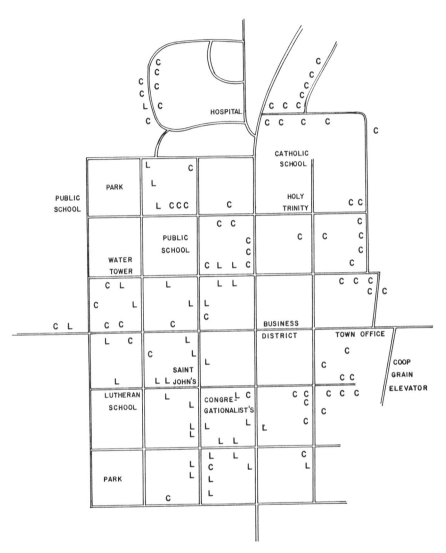

Figure 18. Locations of Catholic and Lutheran residential
units in Okarche Center (compiled from residential listings
in the telephone directory and listings of household
and indivdiuals in church related materials and church
histories).

church and the public schools, and Catholic dominance around the Catholic church and in the hospital area on the north. This places most of the Lutherans in Canadian County and most of the Catholics in Kingfisher County. The distribution illustrates one of the kinds of political problem created by the location of the town. The Lutheran school has never operated a high school, so children of the group go to the public high school. The public schools are supported in part by tax money obtained under county political authority, creating a complex tax relationship in matters of school funding.

The continuation of denominational segregation into the modern era has not been complete, but it has been strong enough to allow the observation that "German," Lutheran and Catholic groups exhibit characteristics associated with "ethnic" units (Barth 1969: 9-38; Whitecotton 1976: 128-9). The German population as a whole was contrasted from the remaining Okarche

population both in cultural content and political
proclivities. But the designation "German" does not
properly represent a functional "ethnicity." This is
because neither the cultural content, including group-
defining symbols, nor the power relations of the Germans
were (or are) unified for the entire population.
Functional ethnicity in the Okarche situation rests on
the level of religious differentiation. Both relations
of power and the symbols which support differentiation
of competitors through time correspond to the congregations primarily, and to the "whole" of the German
population only in a secondary, recent, and superficial
way. Thus, the label "German" implies--using the language of Whitecotton's (1976) discussion of ethnicity--
the "segmentary," and "attributional" characteristics of
ethnic groups, without providing for boundary maintenance, recruitment, or coalition in actions directed at a
resource field. Yet, we may view some strong similarities in the content associated with the two German

church congregations in Okarche. Therefore, it is
convenient to discuss the cultural characteristics of
"Germanness" in Okarche, recognizing that the identification of the German "ethnic group" is tied to two
distinct social populations. Where cultural differences
or distinctive stress-and-response situations exist in
the record, they may be easily pointed out in the
general treatment. In certain areas of cultural content
which serve to symbolize or identify functional social
groups in the community, there is a replication in the
Lutheran and Catholic congregations. It is in these
features, in particular, that continuity of European-
based behavioral patterns is seen.

CULTURAL FEATURES OF GERMAN ETHNIC GROUPS

The characteristics which served to distinguish German in early Okarche from other elements of the population may be divided into two major categories. First, a few cultural features associated with the German population may be thought of as elements derived from heritage which symbolized German identity. Some of these features, such as the Catholic and Lutheran brass bands, family wine-making, the maintenance of segregated seating by generations in the Lutheran church, dedicatory inscriptions and family seating in the Catholic church, and the formation of religious schools represent quite overt differences of cultural practice form the non-German population. These elements sometimes simply define spheres of unified social action, while in other cases they act as "boundary maintaining" features of particular groups. Second, other cultural features associated with the German population represent elements tied to heritage which not only define groups socially, but influence the productive potentials and resource sharing patterns within the community as a whole. These include orientations toward crops, marriage, cooperative enterprise, farmstead organization, and communication (involving both language use and media). The features must be defined largely on a statistical basis, and certain ambiguities arise in the evaluation of their relation to heritage.

Thus, some cultural elements which came to be associated with Germans in Okarche comprised a distinctive "German tradition," an internally defined ideology of "Germanness" on a local level which was quite apart from the total German "cultural system" as it existed in Europe. Other cultural elements involved more subtle differences in orientation which, although they probably arose from the backgrounds of the people, were not incorporated into the endogenous attributional definitions of Germanness in Okarche. These elements served as the basis for "secondary" or exogenous attributions

to the German population. On the level of community-

wide agricultural practice, for example, there were few

differentiating features of the agricultural cycle, crop

selection, or marketing practices which clearly segre-

gated German and non-German farmers. However, Germans

were regarded as "hard-working" and "successful" farmers

by non-Germans, particularly those of the town (see

Willibrand 1951: 288, for an Okarche Times quotation

including images of the Germans as "thrifty" and "law-

abiding" farmers). The productive results of quantita-

tive differences in the scale of farming operations, in

crop diversity, and in numbers of local contacts of the

immediate social spheres in which individuals operated,

lended themselves well to translation into qualitative

judgements. Such positive attributions could also be

adopted by the Germans with ease since the population

changes throughout the early years of Okarche seemed to

indicate the general "success" of German farmers. As we

have seen, however, much of that change resulted from new in-migration of Germans, rather than from an overwhelming failure of non-Germans and displacement by successful German founder-families.

Further, some cultural elements suggesting that German background was important in shaping the community of Okarche did not become prominent until well after the settlement period. This phenomenon has been termed "cultural rebound" in Jordan's (1966: 192-203) treatment of German farming in Texas. The assessment of such situations is difficult because it is not easy to determine how closely an activity is related to cultural proclivities, as opposed to the immediate economic environment or other social conditions influencing the local population. For example, if we suggest that wheat specialization in Okarche (or northwest Oklahoma, for that matter)--a trend which began about the time of the First World War--is a result of the cultural preference of German farmers with a strong background in European grain preferences, we are probably on very weak ground. The local environmental conditions are conducive to specialized wheat production given the certain minimal levels of land holding and agricultural transportation technology. Further, it was the Germans perhaps more than any other group who did not think in terms of specialized farming regimes during the settlement years. On the other hand, commercial butter and cheese production on a large scale also became very important during the First World War period. This was not only well suited to economic circumstances but reflects the intensification of a culturally specific agricultural orientation which was heavily dominated by the German families in Okarche.

It is the specificity and intensity of expression of cultural content tied to German background which is most important in recognizing a "cultural rebound" situation. The contemporary winery is an excellent example of some of the processes involved. Mr. P. Swartz, the owner and

operator of the winery (the only bonded wine producing
operation in the state), is a "second-generation"
Okarchean who learned to make wine from his father.
Family wine production was a minor feature of German
cultural content in Oklahoma during the early part of
this century. As family production waned, local
interest in the wine being made in the Swartz household
taxed the available product and became a mild financial
burden. In order to enter into commercial production,
however, a license and certain major capital investments
were required. The scale of investment in these neces-
sities underscore the personal commitment of the family
to the enterprise, for there was not sufficient real
demand to insure a quick return in profits. Although
the winery was in effect "driven into business," the
product remains tied to a very local market. The establishment of this commercial operation is enterprise out
of a generalized cultural interest. Okarche does not
need a winery, nor is it tied into the larger wine

industry of the United States in a competitive sense. But the winery operates as a reflection of personal and group maintenance of cultural orientation in the context of long-term cultural transformations.

Perhaps the most important differentiating characteristics associated with Germans in early Okarche are (1) continuity on the land after 1900, (2) the initial practice of a generalized farming strategy, and (3) cooperative endeavor in farm production. The first of these characteristics resulted from a tendency of German families to establish ties within their respective religious groups through marriage. Founder and early immigrant families also attempt to assure land holdings for sons by making periodic purchases of land in the region. This continued until land became less available and more expensive. Under specialized wheat conditions of today, it is not economically feasible to continue such a practice. But for the first forty years after settlement, the rule was for family holdings to grow.

The early generalized farming strategy was not unique to
Germans but was manifested strongly in German crop and
husbandry emphasis. This emphasis and the cooperative
structures for butter production, in particular, provided a relatively strong economic orientation and
support system for the younger members of the German
population who took over farms during and after World
War I. Continuity, crop orientation and cooperation,
then, all went hand-in-hand until the years of the
Depression.

Wheat specialization changed this picture dramatically. Although the established German population
remained in control of land in the Okarche area, fewer
but larger farms meant a reduction in the number of
households which might reasonably be drawn into the
farming pattern with generational turnover. There was
an expansion of family interests outside the Okarche
area, then, as young men and women of the community
established new households. Contemporary families have

sons and daughters spread over much of the United States. While there is, of course, tremendous cooperation in producing wheat for sale on national and international markets, the cooperative institutions serve a region in the central-place pattern of Oklahoma. They are, therefore, much less directly tied to the specific population of "German" families, expect by virtue of the numerical prominence of people of German background.

There are still relatively few marriages across denominational lines in Okarche, but the strong pattern of denominational and even congregational marriage preference is no longer in force. The mobility of the young places them in a much wider range of social contacts from the high-school years through the normal marriage ages. University attendance and the acceptance of work outside the community also strongly influence the contemporary marriages of Okarche children. The maintenance of three school systems--Catholic, Lutheran, and Public--tended to segregate children of different

denominations throughout their periods of education.
The closing of the Catholic High School in the 1960's
brought all Okarche teens together during the critical
last four years of their schooling. This has undoubtedly weakened the social differentiation of the Catholic
and Lutheran congregations and served as a major impetus
for social change in the community as a whole.

Religious and non-religious education in the private
schools included a strong emphasis on German during the
settlement period. The language experience of the
Lutherans and Catholics, however, was quite different
(see Willibrand 1951: 286-9). The Lutherans had
relatively great autonomy and commonality in German
background and a general positive experience in German
language use until World War I. The Catholics, on the
other hand, got into a conflict with the bishop in
Oklahoma City over the assignment of non-German priests
in the Oklahoma region. The people still used German
for roughly the same period as the Lutherans. The war

and anti-German sentiment were probably less influential in bringing about the adoption of English than was the generational turnover which occurred between 1915 and 1925. The settler generation spoke German at home and in the community, but their sons and daughters tended to adopt English as a primary language while maintaining German for use with their elders. Following a rather typical United States pattern (see Eichhoff, 1971), the second-generation Okarcheans also learned German through interaction with their grandparents, but dropped regular use of the language with the passing of the settler generation. The third generation and their children have little, if any, knowledge of German as the result of their association with the community.

In summary, it is clear that most of the cultural features which are strongly associated with German background were dropped in a generational turnover process similar to that which brought about a total English language orientation. Yet the major groups defined by

German cultural content in the early community have
remained intact as socially bounded entities through the
present. The group boundaries, however, are by no means
as firm today as they were in the past. It is interesting to note that early settlers of the German-speaking
era are thought of, and to a great extent speak of themselves, in the images of "pioneer" life (see, for
example, the Indian-Pioneer Papers interview of Fred
Schroder, Interview No. 9782, 24 Jan. 1938; and Sunday
Oklahoman, May 30, 1976: A5). In the contemporary
community, the notions of German identity are typical of
American notions of German character. Thus, with a few
exceptions, even in the area of identification of
cultural elements tied to German heritage, the people of
Okarche are not greatly different from other, non-German
Oklahomans.

CHAPTER VI

GENERAL CONCLUSIONS

SUSTANTIVE REVIEW

This study began in an attempt to account for the
nearly exclusively "German" population of present-day
Okarche in the contexts of cultural changes and the
geographic development of Oklahoma. The town and rural
elements of Okarche have been approached through demographic, technological, and social representations, and
a number of specific generalizations pertinent to a wide
array of historical questions have been offered.
Indeed, the summaries of analysis in the three preceding
chapters primarily respond to the long list of working
questions introduced in Chapter I (pp. 14-5). Now it is
necessary to draw the Okarche information into a more
general and abstract frame of reference. We must seek
in the historical development of Okarche those

principles and processes which extend beyond the time-
space limitations of early Oklahoma settlement. In this
way we may answer the central questions of how Germans
succeeded, and at the same time understand some of the
factors which determine differential success of groups
at all times and in all places.

In a brief substantive review we may view the developing patterns of energy control and flow in the rural
development of Okarche as well as the changing patterns
of social and economic interaction of the community.
Our goal is to understand what advantage German background conferred upon families in the early community
and what manifestation of German background meant at
different times to the maintenance or development of the
system of relations on the local level. Because the
boundaries of the system changed through time, we will
also view changes in the "system" to "environment" links
of the Okarche community. That is, viewed from Okarche
the change in systemic boundaries appears as an increase

in the intensity and channelling of information between the community and higher level political-economic units. Thus, we can maintain Okarche as a geographic identity while recognizing the fundamental transformations it has undergone. The review begins with social differentiation in Okarche and then turns to economic development, citing limited demographic trends which are interrelated with social and economic changes.

A simple diagram (Figure 19) illustrates the major relations of the subpopulations of early Okarche. The German-speakers formed two primary groups represented by two levels of hierarchy--the local church and the regional/national church organization. A family had as its primary group of association the congregation of which it was a part, and through which it sometimes received supports from established congregations elsewhere. The interaction across denominational lines was minimal at first, giving way to some economic interaction in the areas of wheat marketing and dairying.

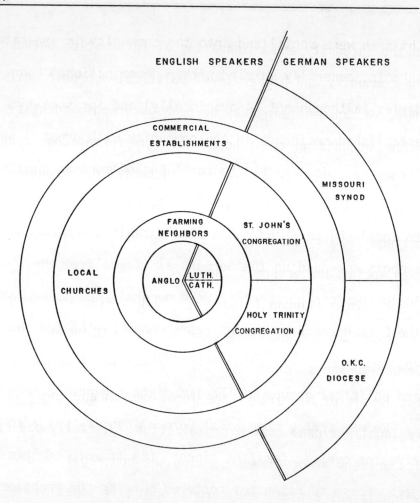

Figure 19, Schematic representation of local and regional social-hierarchic relationships, emphasizing differentation of the English-speaking and German speaking population of Okarche.

Children were socialized into the community in separate schools, generally married within denominational boundaries (although not always locally) and for some time established residence in the community with great frequency. Meanwhile, the rural Anglo-American population was directly linked to farming neighbors, and then to local churches and commercial establishments. The symbols surrounding the Germans as viewed from the Anglo-American perspective were generally positive, and the German resource groups represented by the two church congregations were quite competitive with other social and political groups of the immediate region.

We may state, then, that German identity was adaptive for certain families since: (1) it enabled them to gain access to resources centered outside the frontier community of Okarche, and (2) it provided them with constant formal social ties within the frontier community. The latter point requires further clarification. The church congregations represented local social

resources on a larger scale and more permanent basis
than the farm neighborhood and church ties of the non-
Germans. Immediate farming neighbors changed constantly
during the turnover period; the larger areal coverage of
the congregations helped maintain continuity of associations by people of like interest, while not basing the
association on proximity of homestead locations. Moreover, the fact that German was spoken formally in the
Lutheran church, and at least socially among the
Catholics, aided in regulating membership within the
resource groups each congregation represented. Thus,
under any situation of economic stress we would expect
fewer German failures.

As German farmers expanded their operations by
adding tracts to their homestead land, their sons were
coming of age, marrying, and having children. The
"German identity" of such first generation Okarcheans
was somewhat weaker than that of their parents, but
non-German competition was also weaker. Furthermore,

congregational ties were strengthened by numerous local

marriages, and regional ties were enhanced by marriages

out to other towns (particularly in the case of the

Lutherans). The generational transition, then, marked a

shift to dual-language church services in the Lutheran

church. This potentially opened the church to English-

speaking Lutherans, although its primary impact was to

reduce the differentiation of Lutherans and Catholics on

the basis of language-use patterns. But the basic

relations of the settler generation remained intact

through the generational transition. The enlarged and

growing Catholic and Lutheran congregations remained

strongly bounded from non-German elements of the popula-

tion.

The parallel of technological and language-use

changes in Okarche's history, as noted above, strikingly

fits with the generational transition periods (see

Figure 20). Thus, just as dual-language church services

began with such a transition period--aided perhaps by

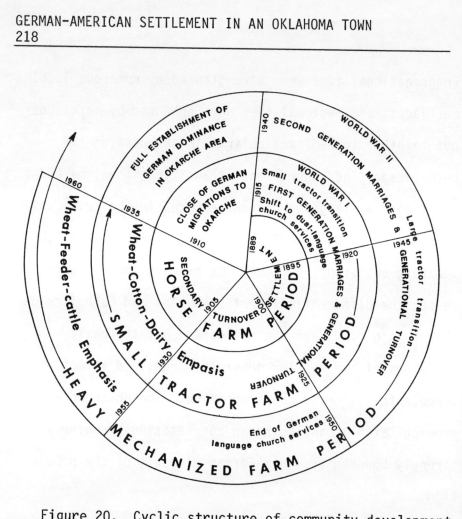

Figure 20. Cyclic structure of community development and generational turnover, including major linguistic, migration, and economic transofmrations of Okarche from 1889 through 1960.

anti-German sentiments of the First World War--regular German-language church services at St. John's ended in the early 1950's. This is a time when the second generation Okarcheans were firmly established as the primary household heads of the region, and persons who were 20 in 1890 had attained the age of 80 years. Indeed, most of the initial adult founders of Okarche were well over 20 in 1890, and few of them remained in the Lutheran congregation in 1950.

On the technological front the generational transitions provided impetus for innovations leading to specialization. Both transitions began during technologically active war periods, when wheat prices also were quite high. Young men taking over their fathers' farms generally had more land to contend with than had their parents, considering that established operations of the post-settlement period involved optimal broken tracts. Thus, even if the acreage turned over to a son were close to the original homestead size, the improved

acres would represent work requirements beyond the
capabilities of a single individual, given constant
technological aids. Still, as we have seen, there was
not a wholesale giving-over to heavy technological
change on the farm. An information model of production,
consumption and work output on a farm with options for
the use of work-animals or tractors aids in pointing out
critical variables in the changing agricultural system.
The model (see Figure 21 for flow diagram) expresses a
number of variable surrounding technical and cropping
decisions, fuel requirements, and the ultimate payoff of
cash over costs. The Oklahoma farmers maintained
limited profit interests initially, but were too dependent upon external commodities to operate totally
sustaining--economically "closed"--farms. However, an
interest in cash is not sufficient to propel a near
subsistence-level farm into a more specialized technological pose. We must presume, then, that individuals
maximized cash production and "land worked per unit of

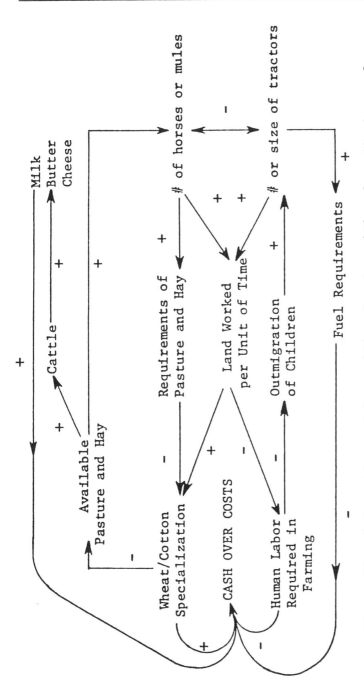

Figure 21. Information model providing for transition from the horse farm to the specialized tractor farm.

time," and that these variables jointly are crucial to the changes of the larger system.

Given these conditions, individuals may be capable of specialization by virtue of both (a) increased land coverage per year, within the limits of available land, or (b) reductions in the human work force. These two alternatives amount to specialization in that both reduce total human work input contributing to the region's yearly production. It should be noted, this is most possible when tractors are employed. Larger tractors will accomplish more work, at a cost in fuel, while reducing or maintaining the size of the required labor force. On a horse-farm, increases in the number of work animals generate requirements of pasture and hay which limit specialization in cash crops. Addition of animals would also increase human labor requirements, not only in working teams, but in hay cutting and husbandry chores. Thus, specialization is highly constrained in the horse-farm system.

The critical variable promoting or retarding specialization on a tractor farm is the cost of availability of fuel. As long as fuel is plentiful and inexpensive, the payoff from specialization in cash crops--even at relatively low prices--may be great. During the introduction of tractors in Oklahoma, the work benefits and fuel costs were probably not as important to farmers as the potential for recommitment of farmland to specialty crops. Later, and particularly after World War II, energy costs continued to decline while production and utilization of gasoline, natural gas, and electricity increased dramatically (see Demand and Conservation Panel of the Committee on Nuclear and Alternative Energy Systems 1978 for a review of pricing and demand in major energy resources). In the long-term, system fuel and work potentials brought about reductions in work animals, and, ultimately, in cattle keeping except as a specialized meat-producing enterprise. An impact on this trend was the reduction of cash from dairying, although the potential losses were more than absorbed by cash from grain or cotton sales. And dairying continued until a situation developed in which labor on individual farms became a critical variable, available technology allowed successful specialization, and the farmers involved were relatively uncommitted to past practices--optimal conditions for the shift occurred during the late 1930's and World War II.

When dairying began to wane, the shift was relatively rapid. The erosion of interest on the part of farmers jeopardized cash gains for individuals contributing to cooperatives such as the one in Okarche. That is to say, it is not simply the "popularity" of a given strategy of farming which always contributes to major shifts of emphasis--the initial decisions of a few individuals may be sufficient to tip the balance of costs and profits against others engaged in an activity.

From these multiple factors of human decisions, technology, market values, and labor conditions were formed the three basic agricultural stances described in Chapter IV and listed in Figure 20. The specific energy flows, intensity of production and consumption, and reinvestment practices for the three periods, reflecting the variables of Figure 21, are depicted in the three diagrams of Figure 22. The predominantly "internal" cycling of energy on the horse farm was an efficient state of affairs, but did not produce large cash gains. As tractors were introduced, the cash output was reinvested in land, and the impact of specialization of human labor requirements was deferred temporarily. Finally, as land cased to be available, pressure was placed on households to become smaller or suffer reductions in income relative to perceived needs in the developing commodity orientations of the nation. In essence, the following means of increasing household income and the per capita income from farming became important, roughly in the sequence presented:

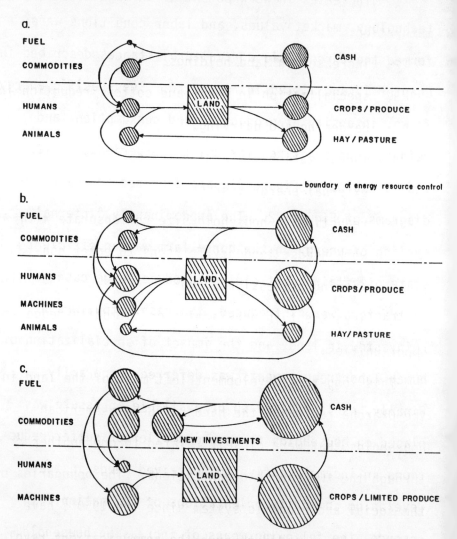

Figure 22. Flow diagram of resources and production during (a) the horse-farm period, (b) the small-tractor period, and (c) the large-tractor period.

1. increases in work potential through household maturation,

2. increases in land holdings,

3. specialization in wheat and cotton; reduction in gardening and dairying,

4. mechanization of farming tasks; diversion to external energy sources,

5. reduction in household size commensurate with work needs; tendency for sons to enter non-farming professions, and

6. investment in non-farming or commodity-hedge opportunities.

This long-term development left most of the land in the Okarche region in the hands of German-American households that were closely related to one another through the two church organizations. The boundaries of the social and economic system since the 1950's have been greatly expanded through the communications revolution of the post-War era. Thus, the geographic locali-

ties of immediate importance incorporate a regional
sphere and a national/international sphere associated
with wheat production. Within the regional sphere (see
Figure 23) are the county seats at Kingfisher and El
Reno, as well as Oklahoma City, all of which provide
shopping and marketing services for farmers. Most
politically important is Oklahoma City. Oklahoma State
University is significant in Okarche, as it has been
since its founding because of its agricultural
programs--very few children from Okarche have gone to
The University of Oklahoma for higher education. The
change in boundary conditions for the community has
impacted the marriage patterns during the modern era,
and even high-school interaction within the Kingfisher/
El Reno/Oklahoma City region is quite strong today.

On the national and international level, Chicago,
Kansas City, and Houston are all important in aspects of
the grain business. Oklahoma City and Houston, as well
as several other cities in Oklahoma and Texas, are

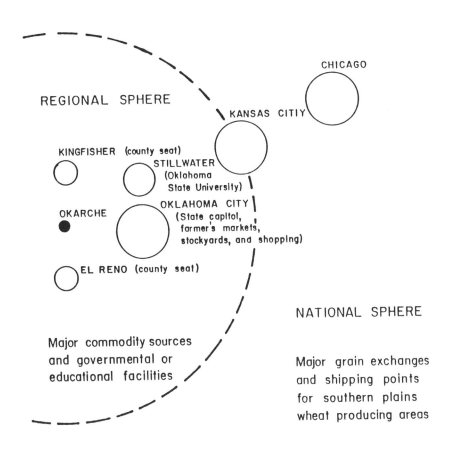

Figure 23. Places of regional, district, and local importance to contemporary Okarche economic activity.

important to the Okarche region because they serve as
headquarters for gas exploration. Property-owner shares
from the production of natural gas in central Oklahoma
represent perhaps the most significant impact on the
economy of the past decade--more indeed, than the real
impact of the Soviet grain deals of recent years. Both
world wheat production and energy supplies should
continue to influence local decision-making and economy
in the immediate future.

ORDER AND DISORDER

The specific events of social and economic development in Okarche exemplify more general processes of
systemic change, especially those of "frontier"
dynamics. We must now directly consider some of these
general processes and attempt to discern what the
Okarche study tells about broad aspects of systemic

change. We may begin with the observation that the total historical development of Okarche seems to involve a progression from (1) a state of affairs characterized by disassociated or highly independent events, to (2) a more regularized, cohesive, or otherwise orderly system. On the demographic front the birth and death rates, migrations, families, and households all develop toward rather stabilized conditions with time. As the settlement era draws to a close there is a decrease in the magnitude of change in the absolute balances of population and the localization of people on the landscape. Social boundaries too, at first multifaceted and poorly defined, become more strongly manifest as familial ties to land, neighbors, and new relations become more coherent. The economic strategies of the town and rural folk are at first not wholly consistent but become attuned to each other with time. And the economy, together with the technology supporting it, becomes adapted to the larger regional and national systems of commodities, transportation, and communication.

The frontier system moves through a series of alterations of state toward essentially stabilized conditions. This development is similar in some respects to ecological succession, although the two processes differ substantially in several important ways. The form of the development may be graphed as follows:

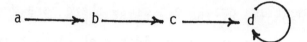

where each state of development represents a different set of relations and intensities of relationship in the areas of demography, social differentiation, agricultural practice, and regional or national ties. The terminal state of such a progression is essentially homeostatic in operation when viewed in the short term. However, this is not meant to imply that any complex social situation may be viewed as homeostatic in the long run. Indeed, demographic, social, and economic

variables do not actually maintain the specific
"equilibrium controls" of the homeostatic model since
there is no explicitly defined value at stake in the
operation of such system of values. Rather, a "stable"
state is achieved by the blind operation of many
variables in the chaotic initial conditions of the
system--the flow of things produce a tendency toward
natural order, even though there is no "teleological"
capacity of the system as a whole. The duration of such
a "stable" state is dependent upon its efficiency in
maintaining energy flow requirements set by its
organization. The efficiency of the system may be taxed
by numerous environmental circumstances, and under
extreme conditions the fundamental relationships of the
"stable" system may be forced to change.

The evolution of an ecosystem (see Odum 1971:
251-75) involves many kinds of trends, the most
important of which concern the relations between
community production (total photosynthesis) and

community respiration (energy yielding biotic oxida-
tion). If the ratio of production to respiration is
greater than one, organic matter accumulates in the
system. This accumulation is the net production
(apparent photosynthesis) of the community. An ecosystem undergoing succession tends toward a balance of
production and respiration, regardless of its initial
ratio, resulting in a large stable biomass, kept within
limits by conditions of climate and soil (Odum 1971:
253-4). Agricultural systems maximize accumulation of
biomass rather than a production/ respiration ratio of
1. They, therefore, retard or inhibit the establishment
of natural energy conserving relationships which characterize climax ecosystems. There is, then, a continual
drain of energetic potential from the agricultural
field-unit which must be replaced if the system is to
maintain a high rate of production.

Thermodynamic order functions of the ecosystem
adjust in succession, then, according to the stability

principle, which states that "any natural enclosed system with energy flowing through it, whether the earth itself or a smaller unit . . . tends to change until a stable adjustment, with self-regulating mechanism, is developed" (Odum 1971: 38). But in the agricultural system ecological stability is obtained only to the extent that human actions are consistent with environmental potentials, and energy drains, in particular, are balanced by inputs from external sources. In temperate climates the control of energy drain and maximization of production of usable plant parts have both been accomplished, although at a high cost of energy and commitment. The intensive use of pesticides, fertilizers, and irrigation, coupled with selection for high-yield crop varieties, produces far reaching effects on soil, groundwater, natural biotic regimes, and people. Indeed, the system is anything but self-regulating. In spite of all the appearance of "stability" under human control, then, the complex agricultural system is

actually a controlled "growth" operation. This makes it
subject not only to ecological stress but also to
economic stress.

Odum (1971: 252) presents a list of ecosystem
characteristics for developing the mature stages of
ecological succession. The list is partially summarized
in Table 8, which also presents a tabular model of
agricultural change from generalized to specialized
farming. The similarities of both farming systems to
the developing natural ecosystem should be immediately
apparent. The community energetics of all of these
systems are similar (items 1-5), and highly contrastive
to the nature ecosystem. All three of these systems are
also relatively "specialized"--they have low indices of
diversity (items 7-10) and rapid, inefficient energy
exchanges (items 14-16 and 19). Finally, all three of
these systems are extremely fragile. Stability (item
20) against external stresses is weak.

Ecosystem Attributes	Early Stages---Mature Stages[a]		Generalized Agriculture---Agribusiness	
	Greater or less than 1	Approaches 1	Greater than 1	increasing
1. Gross production/respiration ratio	Greater or less than 1	Approaches 1	Greater than 1	increasing
2. Gross production/standing crop biomass	High	Low	High	Very High
3. Biomass supported/unit energy flow	Low	High	Low	Very Low
4. Net Community Production	High	Low	High	Very High
5. Food Chains	Linear	Weblike	Intermediate	Linear
6. Total Organic Matter	Small	Large	Large	Small
7. Species Variety	Low	High	Intermediate	Low
8. Species Equitability	Low	High	Low	Low
9. Biochemical Diversity	Low	High	Low	Very Low
10. Pattern Diversity	Poor (tends to randomness)	Well-organized	Poor	Poor
11. Niche Specialization	Broad	Narrow	Narrow	Narrow
12. Size of Organism	Small	Large	Large	Large
13. Life Cycles	Short, Simple	Long, Complex	Short, Simple	Short, Complex
14. Mineral Cycles	Open	Closed	Open	Open
15. Nutrient Exchanges	Rapid	Slow	Rapid	Rapid
16. Role of Detritus in Nutrient Regeneration	Unimportant	Important	Intermediate	Unimportant
17. Production	Quantity	Quality	Both	Both
18. Internal Symbiosis	Undeveloped	Developed	Poorly Developed	Undeveloped
19. Nutrient Conservation	Poor	Good	Poor	Very Poor
20. Stability	Poor	Good	Poor	Poor

Table 8. comparison of ecological succession and agricultrual specialization trends (succession developmental characteristics after Odum 1971: 252-8).

Taken as a sequential development, the trends of
agricultural specialization are antisuccessional,
especially as regards energetics. This is the result of
a number of artificial constraints placed upon the
standing crop biomass. On the community level, the
total biomass standing at any time is reduced as
agricultural is extensified, the variety of organisms
supported in a unit of space is reduced, and the bio-
chemical diversity of the community is reduced. On the
individual level, the size of plants, especially the
usable portions, is maximized. Thus, the usable yield
of the community (net usable production) can increase
even though the total biomass standing in the system is
reduced. Production is both qualitative and quantita-
tive in the agricultural system, depending upon the
selective capacities of the cultivators and the ability
of the technological system to replenish depleted
nutrients. The energy cost of the system is high and
increases much more rapidly than yield. Odum (1971:

412) estimates, for example, that agricultural yields may double with tenfold increases of fertilizer, pesticides, and horsepower. Moreover, fuel powered agro-industry which produces four times the yield of horse-farm agriculture requires 100 times the resource expenditure.

When one views the development of a farming community such as Okarche, then, the critical ecological variables become (1) yearly production, (2) yearly resource expenditure, and (3) efficiency of nutrient regulation. In order to increase or maintain production, increases in yearly resource expenditure are exacted (some local and some external) and the efficiency of extant nutrient regulation mechanisms is taxed (whether natural or artificial). A "stable" system may be largely self-contained on the level of the individual farm, with a consequent cost of productivity per year. Otherwise, a "stable system is subordinated to larger regulatory interests, mainly economic, and

will remain stable only so long as those interests
remain intact. In thermodynamic terms, all agricultural
systems are ecologically entropic, and they increase in
disorderly tendency with intensity. The work of "pump-
ing out" the disorder in these systems is a product of
higher-level order in the human system--technological
capacity, social organization, ideals regulating
consumer patterns. Thus, the development of specialized
wheat agriculture in Okarche and elsewhere is a function
of economic goals of individuals (setting the desired
levels of productivity) operating against fuel-
acquisition technology, fuel-price stability, fuel-use
efficiency, commodity market openness, national consumer
patterns, the efficiency of direct technological application in agriculture, and the ability of farmers to
withstand economic stress from these factors while maintaining at least minimal production. To the extent that
the agricultural system follows the agricultural trends
listed in Table 8, it must be transformed from a system

understandable primarily in ecologic terms (through
energy flows) to one understandable partially in
economic terms (through cash circulation), and partially
in social terms (through rules of resource access and
channeling).

FRONTIER-STABILIZING DEMOGRAPHIC TRENDS

In the preceding section it is argued that developing patterns of energy control and flow involved social
changes within the Okarche community and changes in the
economic articulation of Okarche to larger systems. The
development, it is argued, was necessary to counteract
the energy-inefficient tendencies of the agricultural
system, especially as mechanization under a profit
motive commenced. German identity was adaptive in the
context of the developing community because it allowed
German farmers insurance against failure in the critical

adjustive years of settlement. German background quickly provided a strong factor of "order" in the frontier
system, which facilitated resource access and enhanced
potential economic benefit of its possessors. As energy
requirements and economic commitments changed, external
ties of the local system were expended to counteract
increased "disorder" of the agricultural ecosystem.
Meanwhile, the identifying symbols and behavior of dominant German groups were modified. Both initial social
conditions on the frontier and the social and economic
changes of the post-frontier period were initiated
mainly on a conscious basis. They represent "choices,"
then, even if options within particular historical
circumstances were highly constrained. Therefore, we
must now consider models of the natural stabilizing
trends of the frontier, viewed again as ecological
phenomena. These natural trends tend to limit individual and group options in the changing system.

Social "order" is especially promoted by demographic stability, and the population development of frontiers follows certain regular stabilizing trends (see Lefferts 1977: 47-8, Figure 4). We shall view the gross population trends of the frontier as a self-organizing system tending toward an equilibrium which is a function of applied technology, initial constraints on land acquisition, and environmental potentials. The ideal system would operate in a manner analogous to the relations of production and respiration in the developing ecosystem (see Figure 24a). During ecological succession when productivity exceeds respiration, the net production brings about accumulation of biomass in the system. At climax the biomass is at a maximum, while production and respiration are approximately equal. The level of total development of the system is determined by energy potentials of the initial environment. Similarly, the net accumulation of individual in the frontier system will increase as in-migration and births, or both, exceed

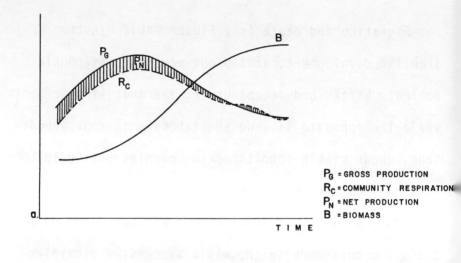

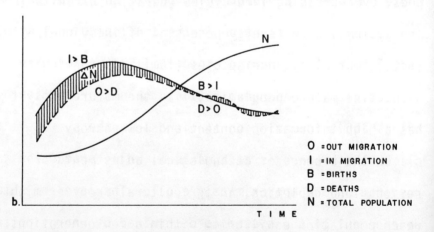

Figure 24. Stabilizing trends of the succession mode (a) and the frontier demographic system (b) (succession mo⸱ after Odum; the frontier demographic system expresses the essential relations of "turnover" and "cumulative inertia"

out-migration and death (see Figure 24b). In the

frontier development, in and out movements of people

dominate births and deaths during the initial stages,

while the opposite is true as stability is approached.

Thus, under stable conditions the population should be

at a maximum, while net and absolute changes in popula-

tion on any time basis remain at a minimum. The system

builds "order" much in the way a successful ecosystem

does, by increasing life-cycles (duration of units in

the system), size (energy potential of individual

units), mutuality, and species (familial) continuity in

situ. The mature population, like the mature ecosystem

has a high information content and low entropy.

In the absence of technological adjustments or

serious land depletion, an agricultural frontier might

reach population equilibrium within a few generations.

Such a development would approximate the age-sex charac-

teristics presumed by stable-population theory (Weiss

1973, Swedlund 1975)--constant age-specific death rates

and perfect replenishment through births. In an actual situation, many kinds of perturbances may effect the development. The size of the frontier, density of settlement, and initial investments of labor and capital by frontiersmen may produce changes in the time required to reach stability. In many cases, technological change will modify the potentials of the system so that the population trends start into secondary or tertiary adjustments. Comparison of frontier patterns provides, in spite of the difficulties of substantive difference, several reliable potential measures of social change and development phenomena (see Thompson 1973; Miller and Steffen 1977). However, the comparison of active processes in frontiers of different developmental rate might be aided by having a means of identifying analogous stages of development in any two systems.

For example, if we take <u>duration of residence</u> on a farming frontier as a measure of successful farm establishment, then a measure of "order" of the system would be the ratio of (1) residents already in the system for some set time (say, one year), to (2) residents of shorter acquaintance in the system. The rate of change of this ratio during the development of a frontier would define the population cycle in such a way that comparison of widely divergent systems would be possible. The observation of a single system using this ratio allows a direct observation of changing information content in the gross demographic system (cf. Odum 1971: 253, Table 4, on "overall homeostasis" in ecosystems).

The population system of Okarche is depicted in Figure 25 as a stability seeking system (a), and through independent estimates of migration, nativity, and mortality inputs (b). The development of the Okarche population matches the "succession" model well, although it reflects perturbances of technological changes after the 1930's. The system became technologically limited with the establishment of the tractor-farm and the trend toward agroindustry, reflected in out-mitgrations and a

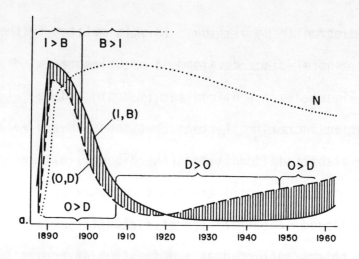

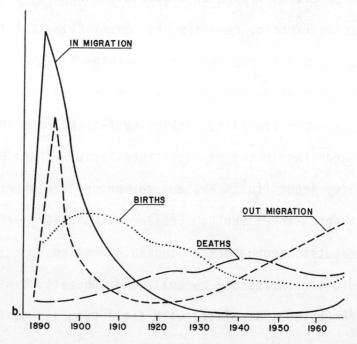

Figure 25. The population system of Okarche depicted as a stability seeking frontier system (a) and through independent estimates of migration, nativity, and mortality

net reduction in population. This is related to the larger central-place development of Oklahoma, as depicted in Figure 26a. The frontier is dominated by population-increasing factors, but tends toward relatively stabilized conditions (the diagonal of the graph represents a ratio of increase/decrease equal to 1). The continued capitalization of agriculture provides a "push" effect reflected as a domination of population-decreasing factors, returning to equilibrium at low absolute and net rates of change. Towns and cities gain or lose population depending upon their place in the central-place structure. Major towns (such as Enid, El Reno, and Kingfisher) maintain relatively high rates of absolute change (turnover) and may experience growth with capital investments. Cities exhibit higher rates of absolute change and are usually committed to net accumulations of people as well. Agriservice towns, such as Okarche, stabilize with small populations and low basic rates of change.

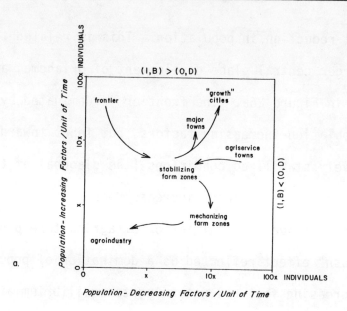

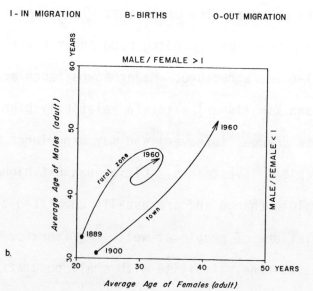

Figure 26. Demographic factors characteristics of central-place development in Oklahoma (a) and age-pattern associations of the rural and town elements of Okarche's population from 1889 through 1960.

The age-pattern associations of Okarche (Figure 26b)
are typical of agriservice towns. Average adult ages on
farms increased from mid-30 to mid-40, where they
stabilized. Meanwhile, the town changed from its very
young beginnings into a center with very large numbers
of retired people, reflected in an average age in excess
of 50. The sexual balances in both cases developed
toward parity, although the town began as female-
dominated and the rural areas were dominated by males.
This sexual balancing reflects the overall stabilizing
trends of the population.

Changing household structures provide the changes of
"continuity," "mutuality," and "size" which characterize
the developing frontier demographic system. Reduction
of turnover increases the information stored in the
demographic system, or increases its "order," on the
level of household units by (1) changing the introduction of new family units in an immediate sense, and
(2) defining the set of households from whom

generational transition will ultimately occur. That is,
reduction of turnover in the frontier period defines the
probable ultimate direction of "continuity" of households. The maturing households achieve greater size and
average-age patterns. This means that both gross and
net work potential (total output and working-age output)
of the units is increased. Expanding friendship and
marriage patterns, as well as segmentation of first-
generation households, contribute to the "mutuality" and
interdependence of the family units.

The high degree of familial variety in the frontier
system limits the economic differentiation of units. As
absolute variety of familial background is destroyed,
however, social and economic variety in the form of
stratification is created. Thus, the "order" in the
population and household system is directly correlated
with the creation of economic order in the community
system--cash and resource flows in the system become
regularized and reasonably predictable in the short

term. As the population system of the frontier

approaches stability, the resource allocation of the

system becomes increasingly well defined. In essence,

familial units carve out sets of resources which they

control, or in which they have a share of control. At a

point when resources become severely limited in relation

of demand, the stable system comes under economic

stress.

RESOURCE AVAILABILITY AND THE FRONTIER

The crucial ecological characteristics of a "fron-

tier" is a high ratio of resources to population. That

is, the frontier per se is a low-density demographic

situation. As the resources of a frontier are tapped

and expended, and as larger population becomes well

established in control of untapped resources, the fron-

tier ceases to exist. At that point, the frontier

becomes either an independent mature system or part of
the system from which its population sprung. As a
geographic/economic entity, then, the frontier possesses
properties which appropriately warrant the often glibly-
used term "safety-valve." It is a zone that will
accommodate population from the crowded core of a
"growth" system, while also augmenting core resources
and providing expansive growth for investment. For the
settlers, a frontier is a land of individual opportunity, while in pure economic terms it is a land of
windfall profit for both local and absentee investors.
In either case, the initial risk may be high, but as
stabilization begins, the risk is dramatically reduced.
Thus, core areas are able to withstand pressures for
internal reorganization, both economic and social, by
virtue of frontier development. At the same time,
however, frontier development brings about changes of
overall scale and "order" in the core-frontier system.

Figure 27 presents characteristics of population

density and mobility, population entropy, and fuel-use

efficiency for frontier development. The graphs may be

employed as either geographic or temporal representa-

tions, depicting (1) regional inter-relationships of

core, developing, and frontier areas, or (2) the

progressive development of a region from its "frontier"

period through a highly "developed" state. The frontier

is opposed to the core in terms of fuel-use efficiency.

Even though the technology of frontier development may

be rudimentary, the release of commodities for local or

core consumption is high in relation to either labor or

capital investment. Indeed, the core consumption of

energy reflects the costs of heavier technology and an

orientation toward manufacturing functions in the

system. In the developing zone, one encounters the

"growth" industry, manifested in a "state of the art"

technology and relatively efficient fuel consumption.

Thus, while both energy consumption and output increase

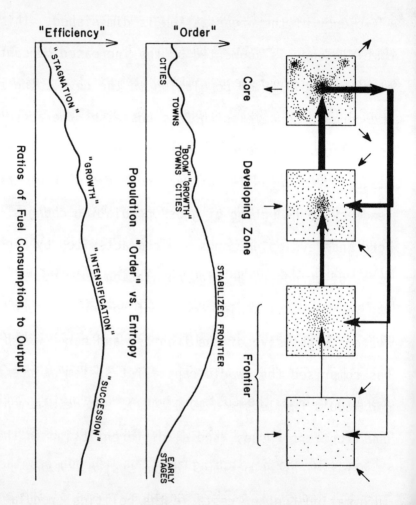

Figure 27. Ideal patterns of population density, mobi
population entropy, and fuel-use efficiency for frontier de
ment,. suggesting temporal relations of frontier systems an
the geographic characteristics of the core-frontier system.

as one approaches the core situation, the productive efficiency of the organization is diminished. This lack of efficiency is augmented by the increased concentration and mobility of population in the developing zone and core. The developing zone possesses the accretional population characteristics of the initial frontier stages (see again Figures 24a and 26a), without the tendency to reduction of gross population changes. The core and developing zones are characterized by high rates of turnover, or high population entropy.

Yet there is a high degree of "order" in such systems, inclusive of the frontier and core, which also has comprised the "world capitalist system" since the mid 1600's (Wallerstein 1975: 401). As development of new frontiers ensues, social differentiation in the form of stratification accrues to the system. A great information content rests in the political regulatory structures of the developing system so that resources are channeled to privileged individuals and away from

the unprivileged. This is a characteristics of high-
density population, such that the ratio of resources to
population remains low (see Wallerstein 1975: 406 on
"ethno-nations" and the political requisites of the
capitalist world-economy).

These characteristics define the importance of
ethnic identity in active local social relationships of
particular "communities" in the system. We have seen in
the study of Okarche that ethnicity, corresponding to
elements of heritage and manifesting in limited "traditional" behaviors and attitudes, was important in the
frontier situation but decreased in importance as the
Oklahoma frontier reached population stability, followed
by regional specialization. Indeed, it is argued here
that German identity was <u>adaptive</u>, or conferred
resource-access advantage to certain families. We may
argue, further, that in any high-risk situation strong
social bounding will serve to limit group resource
drains while maximizing continuity of participants in

sharing networks. In the low-population-density situation of the frontier the most efficient local-resource controls may be those created by "ethnic" identification. Such organizations do not compete well against the more centralized political regulation of differentiation, highly-developed systems, such as that of a "core" area. But they may compete if sheltered by poor core-frontier communications technology. Thus, as the communications technology develops, the "adaptive" value of primarily ascriptive "ethnic" identifications wanes. Ethnic boundaries change to allow access to "free-floating" political-economic resources, if continued "gain" in the post-frontier system is to be obtained (cf. Eisenstadt 1969: 91-2, 361-2; Wallerstein 1975: 406).

What is remarkable is the fact that, in spite of the high rate of regional "production" of a frontier, the position of many frontiersmen in the total system is such that per capita production is low to marginal.

This is also a function of communications technology, largely controlled by the core, which detracts from commodity sales and increases costs of core-produced items. Ethnic identity in frontiers, then, mediates against high risks of frontiersmen who control little capital and are familially isolated in a turbulent demographic system. In the long run, the flexibility of identifying symbols surrounding an "aggregation of people" of common interests determines whether they will (1) succeed in tapping political resources of the developing system, or (2) suffer progressive social and economic isolation which limits sharing in the "growth" system.

We should not be surprised, given the differences in energetic and demographic tendency of frontier and core systems, to find ethnicity as an important feature of highly differentiated systems, especially in the urban arena. It is in the highly stratified core that more and more people are excluded from direct control of resources, and where the risks attendant to survival become critical. Further, it is in the core centers that population turnover is highest--local circulation of people is tremendous, while labor conditions cause high rates of in and out flow. Ethnic identification in these conditions, promoting closure of resource enclaves, keeps the sparse resources of the unprivileged working within proscribed arenas. Ethnicity in these situations is adaptive for the same reasons it is on the frontier--it mediates against high risks of people who control little capital and are familially isolated in a turbulent demographic system. From this point of view, ethnicity is an adaptive pose, centered upon the intensity of aggregations of symbols which identify, socially bound, and behaviorally orient, aggregations of people. Under situations of demographic and economic stress, the symbols will intensify in order to conserve resources controlled by a group, or change in order to obtain resources controlled by others. Under more stable demo-

graphic conditions, or where local competition for
resources is low in spite of turnover of population, the
symbols surrounding a group may decrease in intensity,
or lose their boundary-maintaining functions.

The quality of "ethnic units" is a function of
system size, then, for the complex system pushes ethnic
units toward increased closure and differentiation,
while the frontier system pushes ethnic units toward
decreased closure and differentiation. In essence, the
"melting-pot" so widely heralded in American history is
only one direction of a two-way process, the other
direction of which is a probable eventuality as population strain on the world economy ensues. The production
of a great, unified, middle class in a bounded, capitalist development is the beginning, its social differentiation the end. This presumes, of course, that the
privileged--the elite "ethnicity" of a Marxian economic
core--always resist dispersal of excess resources except
in a limited sense to "co-opt oppositional movement"

(see Wallerstein 1975: 414-5 on the contradictions of

the capitalist world economy).

The adaptive adjustments surrounding ethnicity are

primarily symbolic, as opposed to material, in with

workings. The results of different "ethnic" organiza-

tions on the same landscape, in terms of material

"output," are in many cases "equifinal"--not productive

of adaptive advantage on the part of one group (see Cole

and Wolf 1974; Netting 1977: 93). The adaptive signifi-

cance of ethnicity concerns the amount of resources

maintained and directly controlled vis a vis outsiders

and the total resource field. Thus, an inefficient

system of production which affords high resource

security per capita through time can dominate an

efficient system which affords less individual resource

security.

There is a direct relationship of symbolic change to

the boundary conditions pertaining to a group. The more

well bounded the group, the more intense and rigid the

GERMAN-AMERICAN SETTLEMENT IN AN OKLAHOMA TOWN
264

ethnicity and the more protected the group's resource
base. To the extent that German heritage and traditional symbols in Okarche centered on resource groups,
as has been argued throughout this dissertation, they
worked in precisely this way. Symbols attached to the
German population (or sub-populations), whether autoch-
thonous or externally applied and adopted, delimited a
functional social boundary which regulated resource and
labor flows in the otherwise fluid community-level
system. However, the progressively firm establishment
of German families in the Okarche region, brought by
stabilizing trends of frontier and regional demographic
change, rendered the boundary between Germans and non-
Germans less significant. The symbols of German identity became adaptively neutral. Furthermore, the
primary cultural content associated with German heritage
(language, generalized agricultural practices, maintenance of totally independent schools) was not adaptive
in the long-run development of the larger system.

Softening of local German identity enabled entry into larger-scale interactions necessary for farm and community maintenance. This softening came at points of least resistance, the generational turnover periods, and was facilitated by the adoption of a "Pioneer" ideology which was applied to the early generation of settlers. Indeed, the attributes which were once applied by the Anglo-American population to the Germans are the same as many of those today applied to the Okarche pioneers-- hard-working, religious, family-oriented, efficient farmers.

In the long run, systems of human organization are subject always to the development of energetic potential. People arrive at highly transient adjustments under diverse conditions. Sometimes, as in the case of Okarche, the ability of individuals to persist depends upon their ability to create, mentally, a system or order which will counteract the highly disruptive influences of surrounding events. The community-level

adjustments which arise from these processes of self-
definition may then be further shaped by their techno-
environment contexts. But in the main, those outcomes
we care to call cultures and communities are but parts
of longer-term cycles. As the cycles proceed human
symbols become more rigid, recognized resources more
limited, and potentials inverted. As long as there are
frontiers, the current world-system may continue to
grow in intensity. Without frontiers it must invert
(undergo a technological death) or be transformed into
another kind of system. The problem, of course, is not
a new one; indeed, one account from the West's most
cherished traditions provides a cynical commentary on
social outcomes of such a transformation:

> Thus Joseph acquired all the farm land of
> Eqypt for Pharaoh, since with the famine to
> much for them to bear, every Egyptian sold
> his field; so the land passed over to
> Pharaoh, and the people were reduced to
> slavery, from one end of Egypt's territory to
> the other. Only the priests' land Joseph did
> not take over. Since the priests had a fixed
> allowance from Pharaoh and lived off the
> allowance Pharaoh had granted them, they did
> not have to sell their land. Joseph told the

people: "now that I have acquired you and
your land for Pharaoh, here is your seed for
sowing the land. But when the harvest is in,
you must give a fifth of it to Pharaoh, while
you keep four-fifths as seed for your fields,
and as food for yourselves and your families." "Your have saved our lives," they
answered. "We are grateful to my lord that
we can be Pharaoh's slaves." (Genesis 47:
20-25; in accordance with the New American
Bible text, see Vawter, 1977: 448-50 for
historical commentary).

BIBLIOGRAPHY

Bailey, F. G. 1969. Stratagems and Spoils: A Social Anthropology of Politics. New York: Schocken.

Barth, Fredrik. 1969. Ethnic Groups and Boundaries. Boston, Massachusetts: Little, Brown, and Company.

Braudel, Fernand. 1972. "History and the Social Sciences." In Peter Burke, ed., Economy and Society in Early Modern Europe. New York: Harper and Row.

Cole, John W. and Eric R. Wolf. 1974. Hidden Frontier. New York: Academic Press.

Demand and Conservation Panel of the Committee on Nuclear and Alternative Energy Systems. 1978. U.S. Energy Demand: "Some Low Energy Futures." Science 200 (No. 4338): 142-52.

Eichoff, Jurgen. 1971 "German in Wisconsin." In Glenn G. Gilbert, ed., The German Language in America: A Symposium. Austin, Texas: University of Texas Press.

Eisenstadt, S. N. 1969. The Political Systems of Empires: The Rise and Fall of the Historical Bureaucratic Societies. New York: MacMillan.

Fite, Gilbert C. 1966. The Farmers' Frontier: 1865-1900. New York: Holt, Rinehart, and Winston.

Geertz, Clifford. 1963. Agricultural Involution: The Processes of Ecological Change in Indonesia. Berkeley, California: University of California Press.

Gilbert, Glenn G. (ed.). 1971. The German Language in America: A Symposium. Austin, Texas: University of Texas Press.

_____. 1972. Linguistic Atlas of Texas German. Austin, Texas: University of Texas Press.

Gittinger, Roy. 1939. The Formation of the State of Oklahoma, 1803-1906. Norman, Oklahoma: The University of Oklahoma Press.

Gray, F. and H. M. Galloway. 1959. Soils of Oklahoma. Oklahoma State University Experiment Station Miscellaneous Publications, No. 56. Stillwater, Oklahoma.

Greven, Philip J., Jr. 1970. Four Generations: Population, Land, and Family in Colonial Andover, Massachusetts. Ithaca, New York: Cornell University Press.

Hale, Douglas. 1975. "European Immigrants in Oklahoma: A Survey." Chronicles of Oklahoma, 53 (No. 4; Summer): 179-203.

Hammel, Eugene A. and Peter Laslett. 1974. "Comparing Household Structure over Time and between Cultures." Comparative Studies in Society and History, 16: 73-109.

Harris, David R. 1969. "Agricultural System, Ecosystem, and the Origins of Agriculture." In Peter J. Ucko and G.W. Dimbleby, eds., The Domestication and Exploitation of Plants and Animals. New York: Aldine.

Harris, Marvin. 1968. The Rise of Anthropological Theory. New York: Thomas Y. Crowell Company.

Hartz, Louis. 1964. The Founding of New Societies. New York: Harcourt, Brace, and World.

Haurwitz, Bernhard and James Austin. 1944. Climatology. New York: McGraw-Hill.

Haystead, Ladd and Gilbert C. Fite. 1955. The Agricultural Regions of the United States. Norman, Oklahoma: The University of Oklahoma Press.

Homans, George C. 1942. English Villagers of the Thirteenth Century. Cambridge, Massachusetts: Harvard University Press.

Hudson, John C. 1977. "Theory and Methodology in Comparative Frontier Studies." In D. H. Miller and J. O. Steffen, eds., The Frontier: Comparative Studies. Norman, Oklahoma: The University of Oklahoma Press.

Jordan, Terry G. 1966. German Seed in Texas Soil. Austin, Texas: University of Texas Press.

Kertzer, David I. 1977. Historical Demography and Household Structures: Toward a Better Analytical Framework. Paper presented to the symposium on historical and anthropological demography, Annual Meeting of the American Anthropological Association, Houston Texas, December 1, 1977.

Kuchler, A. W. 1964. Manual to Accompany the Map: Potential Natural Vegetation of the Coterminous United States. American Geographical Society Special Publication No. 36. New York: American Geographical Society.

Lefferts, H. L., Jr. 1977. "Frontier Demography: An Introduction." In David H. Miller and J.O. Steffen, eds., The Frontier: Comparative Studies. Norman, Oklahoma: The University of Oklahoma Press.

Levi-Strauss, Claude. 1966. The Savage Mind. Chicago:
The University of Chicago Press.

Lockridge, Kenneth A. 1970. A New England Town: The
First Hundred Years. New York: W. W. Norton and
Company.

Lowie, Robert H. 1963. Indians of the Plains. Garden
City, New York: The Natural History Press.

Malin, James. 1935. "The Turnover of Farm Population
in Kansas." Kansas Historical Quarterly, 4:
339-372.

Margolis, Maxine. 1977. "Historical Perspectives on
Frontier Agricultural as an Adaptive Strategy."
American Ethnologist, 4 (No. 1): 42-64.

McReynolds, Edwin C. 1964. Oklahoma: A History of the
Sooner State. Norman, Oklahoma: The University of
Oklahoma Press.

Miller, David H. and Jerome O. Steffin (eds.). The
Frontier: Comparative Studies. Norman, Oklahoma:
The University of Oklahoma Press.

Naramore, R. 1973. "Ethnicity on the American
Frontier: A Study of Czechs in Oklahoma." Papers in
Anthropology, 14 (No. 1; Spring): 104-14.

Netting, Robert McC. 1977. Cultural Ecology. Menlo
Park, California: Cummings.

Odum, Eugene P. 1971. Fundamental of Ecology. Third
Edition. Philadelphia, Pennsylvania: W. B. Saunders
Company.

Oklahoma Water Resources Board. 1975. Oklahoma
Comprehensive Water Plan. Report submitted in
fulfillment of legislative directive given in Senate
Bill 510 of the 1st session, 34th Legislature of the
State of Oklahoma. Oklahoma City: Impress Graphics.

Oliver, Symmes C. 1962. "Ecology and Cultural
Continuity as Contributing Factors in the Social
Organization of the Plains Indians." University of
California Publications in American Archaeology and
Ethnology, 48 (No. 1). Berkeley, California:
University of California.

Petrowsky, Clarence L. (ed.) 1974. Missouri Synod
Lutheranism in Oklahoma: 1890-1974. Weatherford
press.

Powell, Sumner Chilton. 1963. Puritan Village: The
Formation of a New England Town. Middletown,
Connecticut: Wesleyan University Press.

Pulte, William J., Jr. 1971. "German in Virginia and
West Virginia." In Glenn G. Gilbert, ed., The German
Language in America: A Symposium. Austin, Texas:
The University of Texas Press.

Rister, Carl C. 1942. Land Hunger: David L. Payne and
the Oklahoma Boomers. Norman, Oklahoma: The
University of Oklahoma Press.

Ruth, Kent. 1976. Eine Kleine Geschichte. Oklahoma
Today, 26 (No 4): 10-12.

Spencer, Robert F. and Jesse D. Jennings. 1977. The
Native Americans: Ethnology and Background of the
North American Indians. New York: Harper and Row.

Stallings, H. C., Stallings, and F. Conover. 1964.
Lutheran Cemetery. An alphabetical list of 196
names, recorded in a complete canvass of all legible
temporary markers and permanent gravestones in the
Lutheran Cemetery, Canadian County, Oklahoma, located
near the town of Okarche. D.A.R. collection
Manuscript: Oklahoma Historical Society.

Steward, Julian H. 1955. Theory of Culture Change:
Methodology of Multillinear Evolution. Urbana,
Illinois: University of Illinois Press.

Turner, Frederick Jackson. 1961. Frontier and
Sections: Selected Essays of Frederick Jackson
Turner. Englewood Cliffs, New Jersey:
Prentice-Hall.

Thompson, Stephen I. 1973. Pioneer Colonization: A
Cross-Cultural View. Reading, Massachusetts:
Addison-Wesley Modular Publications.

Vawter, Bruce. 1977. On Genesis: A New Reading. New
York: Doubleday and Company.

Wallerstein, Immanuel. 1974. The Modern World System:
Capitalistic Agriculture and the Origins of the
European World-Economy in the Sixteenth Century. New
York: Academic Press.

_____. 1975. "Rise and Future Demise of the
World Capitalist System." Comparative Studies in
Society and History, 16: 387-415.

Whitecotton, Joseph W. 1976. "Tradition and Modernity
in Northern New Mexico: An Introduction." Papers in
Anthropology, 16 (No. 2, Fall)

Willey, Gordon R. 1966. An Introduction to American Archaeology: Volume One: North and Middle America. Englewood Cliffs, New Jersey: Prentice-Hall.

Williams, Glyn. 1978. "Industrialization and Ethnic Change in the Lower Chubut Valley, Argentina." American Ethnologist, 5 (no. 3): 618-631.

Willibrand, W.A. 1950. "German in Okarche, 1892-1902." Chronicles of Oklahoma, 28 (No. 3; Autumn): 284-91.

_____. 1951. "In Bilingual Old Okarche." Chronicles of Oklahoma, 29 (No. 3; Autumn): 337-54.

Documents and Census Materials

Indian Pioneer Papers
1938   An Interview with Fred Schroder, Okarche, Oklahoma. Compiled by Nora Lorrin as Interview Number 9782, available in the Phillips Collection of the University of Oklahoma Library (other interviews of local interest are in the collections, although the Schroder interview is the only one of a major early household head of the Okarche community).

Okarche Times
1892   An English-language newspaper published in Okarche, Oklahoma.

1918   An incomplete run of this paper is available on microfilm at the Oklahoma Historical Society newspaper room.

Oklahoma Territorial Census
1890   Manuscript schedules of this territorial
        census are available on microfilm at the
        Oklahoma Historical Society. The same
        information is also stored in a card file in
        the Historical Society Reading Room.

Oklahoma Volksblatt
1903   A German-language newspaper published in
        Oklahoma City and

1909   El Reno, Oklahoma. This was the major
        German-language paper for the Okarche
        population. A nearly complete six-year run
        of this paper is available on microfilm at
        the Oklahoma Historical Society newspaper
        room.

Tract Book Oklahoma
1956   Roll #2, Bureau of Land Management, United
        States Department of the Interior, Records
        Improvement Microfilm. Washington, D. C.
        This document provides basic homestead
        information for the Oklahoma Unassigned Lands
        and other areas homesteaded through 1906.
        The microfilm versions of the book are
        available in the Oklahoma Historical Society
        Reading Room.

Twelfth Census of the United States
1900   Manuscript Schedules of the Twelfth Census of
        the United States are available at the
        national records center in Fort Worth, Texas.
        Microfilms are also available at the Oklahoma
        Historical Society and at Oklahoma State
        University.

1901   Twelfth Census of the United States, Part I,
        Population. Official Report of the 1900
        census. Washington, D. C.

1902   Abstract of the Twelfth Census, 1900.
        Official Report of the 1900 census.
        Washington, D. C.

1903   Twelfth Census of the United States:
        Statistical Atlas, Official Report of the
        1900 census. Washington, D. C.

INDEX